# Enlightenment for Beginners

also by Graham Irwin

A Farm Of Our Own:
a spiritual journey running a smallholding

# Enlightenment for beginners

by
Graham R Irwin

**CityScape Books**

First published in 2001

© copyright, Graham R Irwin, 2001

*All rights reserved. No part of this book
may be reproduced, stored in a retrieval system
or transmitted in any form or by any means,
electronic, electrical, chemical, optical, mechanical,
photocopying, recording or otherwise
without permission in writing from the Publisher.*

**British Library Cataloguing-in-Publication Data**

A catalogue record for this book is available from the
British Library

ISBN 0-9533331-5-9

Published by CityScape Books
PO Box 16554, London SE1 5ZS
www.cityscapebooks.co.uk

Printed and bound in Great Britain by
Biddles Ltd: www.biddles.co.uk

*To Heather, my greatest teacher*

❖

# **CONTENTS**

Introduction ......................................... 9

Enlightenment ....................................... 13

The Nature of God .................................. 18

Openness ............................................ 21

Reincarnation ....................................... 24

Self Esteem ......................................... 27

Change .............................................. 32

The Present ......................................... 35

Love ................................................ 38

Responsibility ...................................... 42

Integrity ........................................... 47

Judgement ........................................... 50

Relationships ....................................... 54

Giving and Receiving ................................ 58

Abundance ........................................... 61

Forgiveness ......................................... 63

Trust and Fear ...................................... 68

Balance and Disease .............................. 73

Free Will ........................................ 76

Mirror Principle ................................. 80

Thoughts Create ................................. 83

Words and Affirmations .......................... 87

Consequences .................................... 91

Unity ........................................... 95

Ego and Attachment .............................. 98

Life Purpose .................................... 102

Peace ........................................... 106

Intuition and Creativity ........................ 109

Angels .......................................... 112

Prayer and Meditation ........................... 116

Inspirational Quotes ............................ 124

❖

# Introduction

Whether we realise it or not, life for all of us is a spiritual journey. However, there is no map for our journey, and each of us has our own particular quest — we just have to work it out as we go along! If we allow it to be so, it can be a journey of excitement, discovery and enlightenment; on the other hand we can make it dull, fearful and heavy-going. The choice is ours, and we can make that choice — and even change our minds — at any time. Once we open ourselves to the infinite range of possibilities the universe has to offer and stop limiting ourselves by our often simplistic human understanding, once we accept that there are things in the universe we cannot yet comprehend or explain, we begin to find that life has so much more to offer than we could ever have imagined.

This book has been inspired by my dear friends with whom I wanted to share my spiritual beliefs. No, on second thoughts, 'beliefs' would be the wrong word; there comes a time when a belief or a trust becomes more than that — it becomes part of oneself, a truth. This book then contains my truths; not necessarily yours, although hopefully some of the ideas and beliefs will stimulate you in developing and refining your own set of truths. Writing this book has in itself been a great learning experience for me and part of my journey of enlightenment. It is often said that we teach what we most need to learn. Leaving aside the point that I don't believe I am here to 'teach' anything to anyone, that I am simply a channel for the messages contained here, many of the lessons in this book have been as much a revelation for me as I hope they will be for you, beloved reader.

This is not about religious beliefs, for I subscribe to no particular religion. However, I do recognise there are many truths in all of the world's major religions. Religions have been created by mankind — and they have often been distorted by him over the ages for his own particular reasons, usually to exercise control over his followers.

I hope the messages contained in this book will help pave the way for anyone who is open to them to find the path of 'enlightenment', whatever that means to the individual personally. I don't say this in vanity, for none of the truths in this book are new — the final section of inspirational quotes is intended in part to show that many of the truths expressed here are not original and are, indeed, as old as the hills. Nor I do I pretend this is the complete story because we all continue to learn and grow throughout our lives.

A number of different headings came to me as I was writing this book, which you will see as chapter headings. As I continued to write I realised that some of these were rather arbitrary — albeit still useful — divisions. Some of the truths could have appeared in any of a number of chapters, and indeed some are repeated in more than one. This is not necessarily a book to read from cover to cover — although you may use it that way if you wish. On the other hand you may find it more useful to pick topics at random, or read those that particularly appeal to you and come back to the others later.

This is more than just a book of theoretical ideas. It includes practical examples — usually fictionalised, but many of them based on real life — for each of the topics covered, as well as the opportunity to experience and practise the topics in your own life using the exercises provided. Enlightenment is not a 'spectator sport'. You cannot learn spirituality from a book. It is something that comes from within each and every one of us; something we must *experience*. It takes time and practice, so please participate as well as read.

I suggest you keep a notebook with you in which to do the exercises. You may also wish to use your notebook to jot down any key points, anything that 'speaks' to you, whether it is something with which you particularly agree or violently disagree. Perhaps you might want to use different coloured pens for those things you agree with and those with which you disagree. Alternatively, or in addition, you may wish to make notes in the book itself (provided it's your own copy!)

You may also find it helpful to play some soft background classical or 'new age' music whilst you are reading the text and doing the exercises. Music activates a different part of the brain which can assist the process of assimilation. However, this is only a suggestion, and there may be times when it suits you to play some soft music and other occassions when you prefer quiet. That's fine; whatever works for you.

Another way to get more from the process is to find a friend to work with — a 'buddy', someone with whom to read the book and work through the exercises together, or who has already been through a similar process. You don't need to show them your exercises (unless you want to), but you may find it helpful to discuss what you are experiencing during the exercises, anything you are having difficulty with, and especially what you have learned. Be prepared to challenge each other, to look deeper within yourselves, examine your motives, help and encourage one another, offer and receive support when you are 'blocked' or resistant and learn from the other's experiences. However, be careful not to get drawn into each other's self-deceptions and justifications.

I truly hope that however you decide to use it, the material that follows may assist you to find insights that will help you lead your life, dear one, with greater love, compassion and trust, and with less fear and doubt. Please take from it whatever speaks to your heart, find your own truths within these pages, and use them, as well as those messages that do not resonate with you, to create your own reality.

In love and light<br>
Graham Irwin<br>
January 2001

# Enlightenment

So you're seeking enlightenment? Where to begin?
There is only one place to begin any journey — and enlightenment, like life, is a journey. The place to start is where you are right now. Begin with the recognition that you already know the answers you are seeking, but are simply pretending not to know or have forgotten.

Start by understanding the apparent paradox that you are alone on this journey, and yet you are one with everything and everyone else in the universe. Acknowledge that you are a divine being, part of All That Is, created in the image of God — whatever you may consider him, her or it to be. Know that it is all that has gone on in your life before this moment that has brought you to where you are now, that there is a purpose for everything. Rejoice in every obstacle you have faced in your lifetime, and bless it as the gift and opportunity it certainly has been to enable you to grow. Remember that the only thing that stands between you and your goals, your heart's desires, your greatest wishes, enlightenment — is YOU... and your fears!

Commit to face life in the truth that every moment is an opportunity to create a new reality — now, and in every moment — based on the infinite possibilities of what can be, not on your fears of what has happened in the past. Know that your successes and your happiness are limited only by what you believe is possible, and that the range of possibilities is only restricted by your limited human understanding. And trust that the universe will show you the answers when you are open to receive them.

Now perhaps some of these ideas are new to you, perhaps

you want to reject them as nonsense, as impossible. That's great! Firstly, you don't have to accept anything — in this book or elsewhere in life — that doesn't resonate with you. You can accept or reject any ideas you choose. However, suppose you suspend your judgement for a while and accept that there might be something in these ideas, even if it's not clear right now what or how or why? As you continue your journey of enlightenment and self-discovery, you may find some of those things that made no sense at the time begin to seem possible — and perhaps even probable.

What is important, however, is that you apply yourself to the subject with an open mind, and an open heart. Rejecting everything out of hand just because it doesn't make sense now will not lead to enlightenment in any form.

You may wish to ask your guides to help you to receive the information with an open heart and to help you learn the lessons that are important for you. We all have guides in the spirit and other unseen kingdoms, in different dimensions. As we continue on our journey we may find that our guides may make their presence felt in some way.

Everyone's path is different, so don't assume that what works for someone else will necessarily work for you, or vice versa. You will need to find for yourself those things that work for you, and those that don't. You will also find the speed of the journey and the timing of events in everyone's lives will vary. It is important not to give yourself a hard time just because events are not unfolding as quickly as you think they should, or that your experiences are different from someone else's.

Enlightenment means getting in touch with our higher consciousness. It means letting go of old beliefs and fears, releasing old ways of being, and doing, and thinking — ways with which we may have been comfortable for most of our lives, but which no longer serve us. It means accepting responsibility for our lives and accepting the power we already have; and by this I mean not power over others but power over ourselves.

It is not an intellectual exercise. The mind can be a barrier to spiritual enlightenment. We are called on to *experience* our lives, not to contemplate them. You will need to start looking deep within yourself to find those things that are keeping you in the past. You will need to face up to your fears before you can let them go and move on. It will certainly get uncomfortable at times. Remember, there is no growth without risk; and enlightenment is about growth — in love, understanding, trust and compassion. You are perfect just the way you are; however, if you wish to grow in love and in light you need to be prepared to put yourself into situations that will stretch you, when you will feel uncomfortable. The fact is, they are only unpalatable to yourself, not to anyone else. There will be times when you need to face up to some apparently unpleasant truths. There is nothing to be gained by trying to deceive yourself. Taking the easy option does not lead to growth and enlightenment. So, are you ready to take a risk, to take yourself on?

There are no gurus, no teachers and pupils. We are, each of us, our own guru; and we are all both teacher and pupil. Just as we teach, so we learn; the two go hand in hand. Just as the only way for us to receive is to give; the only way to be loved is to give away our love; the only way to gain forgiveness is to forgive. And we must also remember to love, honour, respect and forgive ourselves as well as others.

It can be difficult to make this journey of self-discovery and enlightenment alone. It can be hard enough anyway, so you might wish to make the journey with a special friend (or friends), join a support group, or perhaps attend courses or workshops in personal development. Most likely a combination of all of these will suit most people best. Whatever you decide, enjoy it. Once you start the journey — and the fact that you're reading this now suggests you've already begun — you will not want to stop. You will find that, despite the discomfort you will almost certainly feel from time to time, you will want to keep up the momentum. And remember, true friends are those who tell you what you need to hear, not what you want to hear, so choose your friends carefully.

Remember, it's a journey. Enjoy the travelling. And don't forget to smell the roses on the way!

## Example

The following chart is a simple mind map designed to show one interpretation of the interrelationships between the main topics covered. As you read through the book, you may find it helpful to create your own mind map linking the topics and ideas in whatever way seems appropriate for you.

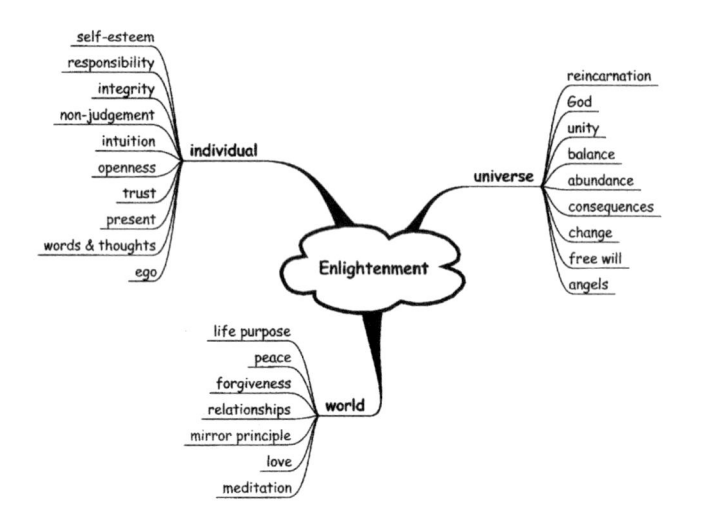

```
                                    Enlightenment
```

**individual**: self-esteem, responsibility, integrity, non-judgement, intuition, openness, trust, present, words & thoughts, ego

**universe**: reincarnation, God, unity, balance, abundance, consequences, change, free will, angels

**world**: life purpose, peace, forgiveness, relationships, mirror principle, love, meditation

## Exercise

Before reading further, take your notebook and a pen, find a quiet area and make yourself comfortable. Put on some quiet music, too, if you want. Take four or five deep breaths; breathe in as far as you can, hold your breath each time for a few seconds and then breath out slowly. Relax your body and quieten your mind.

Take your time over this exercise. It will help you gain some clarity about what it is you want to get out of reading this book as well as from life, and your commitment to seeking it. There are no right or wrong answers, so be honest with yourself.

First of all, write down what enlightenment means to you. To help you think about it, here are some questions; however, do not limit yourself to just these, they are to help you stretch rather than restrict your thinking. What is it you're seeking? How will you know when you get there? Why are you seeking it? What difference will it make to your life? How will it affect others? What is it not? How much do you desire it? What are you prepared to do to achieve it? What are you prepared to give up? What are you not prepared to give up? How much time are you prepared to spend on this venture? How did you get to where you are now? What made you choose this book? What do you make of what you have read so far?

When you have finished, if you are working with a friend or buddy you may wish to share some of your thoughts and any insights you have gained.

❖

# The Nature of God

Personally, I have always had some difficulty with the concept of a God that needs or expects to be worshipped. What sort of God could that be? It sounds more like some deity with an ego the size of a planet, or one that is so insecure that he/she/it needs us to keep telling him/her/it how wonderful he/she/it is! Of course, we may *choose* to worship our God, which is quite a different matter.

A God that loves us all and yet sits there judging us as to whether we will go to heaven when we die or shall be eternally damned in hell on the basis of a few years life on this funny little planet we call Earth? How could someone that loves us ever condemn us to eternal damnation? Or a God that sends his only son as a sacrifice for our sins? Why only one son — surely God could have as many sons as he wants? And if he's God, surely he can forgive us anyway without having to make such a gruesome sort of sacrifice! A God that requires us to mutilate part of our anatomy, something he/she/it gave us in the first place? A God that appears to prefer one race, one gender or one section of humankind over another?

No, there is something not quite right about all this. The idea that there is some greater power than me — fine. But all this control stuff — no way! Somewhere along the line it seems as though the truth has become corrupted as a means of telling us what we should and should not do. And that's another thing — why would God wish to give us free will and then tell us how to run our lives?

I do not wish to suggest that Jesus did not exist, that he was not a great spiritual teacher and healer, or that his death was not — in some way that is hard to explain or understand — to the profound benefit of all humankind. On the contrary. However, I do believe his position in the 'hierarchy' has been misunderstood or misrepresented by the church authorities and religious leaders, just as hands-on healing has been relegated to a very minor part of the Christian church's activity, just as many Christian festivals were timed to fit in with those of existing religions, and just as certain books were apparently arbitrarily included or excluded within the New Testament.

My view of God is not of a patriarchal — or matriarchal — figure sitting in judgement over us all, granting the prayers and wishes of those he or she favours, or deciding what kind of lives each of us will have on Earth. That is, I suggest, a very limiting view of God. I wish to suggest that God is All That Is. All of nature, all of humankind, all life forms, all of the planets, all that is seen and unseen, the entire universe.

The Bible tells us that God created us in his own image (Genesis 1:26). Unfortunately, this statement often appears to be misinterpreted and taken the opposite way round so that we accredit human attributes to God, denigrating both God and humankind in the process. Just suppose the Bible is correct and we are an image — a small but indispensable part — of God? What if we are, at our essence, perfect, whole, complete, all-knowing, immortal?

In this vast universe we live in, the size and extent of which we are unable to measure or even comprehend, it seems inconceivable that our tiny little planet is the only one to contain any form of life. In our own galaxy there are estimated to be in the order of 100 billion stars, each of which like our own sun has the potential to support a number of planets; and there are billions of other galaxies outside our own. With numbers like these, the chance of there *not* being other life forms must be infinitesimally small. It seems gross arrogance to assume that humankind is the only sentient life form in the entire universe, or even that it is the most advanced or intelligent species.

Who can view the miracle of nature, of our own lives, all

living creatures, plants, minerals, mountains, rivers, oceans, the weather, art, the vast expanse of the solar system without a sense of awe? And if all of creation is God itself, how can it be anything other than perfect? And does not this teach us to respect all life forms whether animal, plant or mineral, whether seen or unseen?

### Exercise

Take a look around your home. Look carefully in each room among your possessions — your trophies, books, CDs, ornaments, software, clothes — and find something that has some particular meaning or value to you — not necessarily any monetary value, but something to which you feel some attachment. You will know instinctively when you find the most suitable object, so take your time.

Once you have found it, take the object and give it away; perhaps to a charity shop, a friend who has always admired it, a homeless person, leave it in a park where someone will find it, or bury it somewhere. How you dispose of it will depend on the item and what your intuition tells you. However, be careful not to make a judgement about the value the recipient might place on the object.

The purpose of this little exercise is for you to experience a sense of sacrifice, which is why it is important the item you choose is not something you would have given to a charity shop or jumble sale in any event. It is a helpful way to demonstrate your commitment to the path of enlightenment.

You may wish to make a note in your notebook of any thoughts and feelings that came to you during this exercise. How did you find the special item? How resistant were you to giving it away? If you wish to share your thoughts and insights with your special friend feel free to do so.

❖

# Openness

Most of us probably wish to be viewed as someone who is open. It certainly sounds better than being closed, but what do we really mean by being open? Openness is the degree to which we are willing to accept something; it may be a new idea or experience, a new relationship, praise, constructive criticism, help or assistance, changing old habits or ways of being. Of course, we may well be at the same time open to certain things but not to others.

Ways in which we might show our lack of openness include: arms folded across the chest, an unwillingness to look other people in the eye, an immediate rejection of a new idea or suggestion.

Very often, a perceived downside to being open, and one that we might use as an excuse for a lack of openness, is that we also make ourselves vulnerable. But vulnerable to what? Somehow openness is usually seen as a positive trait whilst being vulnerable is often viewed as undesirable. In fact, openness and vulnerability are really one and the same thing. The difference lies in the result — or rather in our intent. If, for example, we are open to the possibility of a new relationship in our lives, we might attract the kind of relationship we *think* we want — loving, caring, trusting, honest — or we may attract one where the other person is selfish or deceitful or abusive or dishonest. The thing is that openness requires a good degree of trust. Trust that whatever happens in our lives is for the best, even if it does not seem that way at the time. Many adversities that occur in our lives are really blessings in disguise.

The path of spirituality invites us to be open and trusting

in both a 'giving' and 'receiving' sense. Withholding either can make our path rather slower and more difficult.

---

### Example

In the early days of personal computing, two competing systems were being developed with little idea of the impact they were later to have on the world. One of the developers decided to adopt an 'open' design allowing other companies to manufacture components that were compatible with the original and even enabling others to assemble complete 'clone' PCs, perhaps even improving on the original design. The other developer, wishing to protect his design, adopted a proprietary approach keeping a close control on component suppliers and retaining sole manufacture of the computers. The result? A plethora of companies started manufacturing 'clone' PCs, driving down the cost of the machines and encouraging software companies to develop more and more programs to run on the new machine. The low prices and the wealth of software available made the PC popular with users and generated millions and millions of sales. The competing system, which many would argue was a better, more robust system, won a number of adherents. However, with its monopoly, the price remained high and the variety of software available was more limited and there were times when the company struggled to survive. If there is a moral t this tale, I leave it to you, dear reader, to draw your own conclusions. Neither company was 'right' or 'wrong'; but, perhaps had they taken a different approach we would now all be using Apple Macs rather than IBM-compatible PCs.

### Exercise

Find yourself somewhere to become quiet and relaxed. Play some background classical or new age music if you wish and perhaps light a candle. Sit comfortably and take a deep breath. Breathe in as far as you can and hold your breath for a few moments; breathe out slowly. Repeat this several more times, each time allowing your body and your mind to become more and more relaxed.

Now take your notebook. One at a time, take a look at each of the ideas listed below. Try not to look forward; use a piece of paper or a bookmark to hide those items you've not yet come to, and write down your first impression about each one in turn. What do you feel about the idea? Is it a possibility? A probability? A possibility with certain reservations? A certainty? Utter nonsense? Notice also how you feel about each one. Do you feel angry? Happy? Bemused? Did you want to laugh? Did you get a knot in your stomach? Write down everything that you can about your reaction to each point before moving on to the next.

- reincarnation
- life on other planets
- the existence of angels
- the existence of fairies
- Earth has been visited by beings from outer space
- we are spiritual beings first and foremost and human beings second
- astrology
- animals have intelligence
- animals have intelligence at least as great as that of humans
- telepathy
- the ability of some people to communicate with angels and other spirits
- the tarot.

Review your comments. How many of them did you write off as an absurdity? How many times did you feel angry? Or did you want to laugh? There are no 'right' answers. However, your reactions indicate the degree to which you are open to possibilities that are possibly outside your present experience.

If you are working with a companion you may wish to compare notes.

# Reincarnation

Perhaps one of the most fundamental concepts to grasp is that of reincarnation; the idea of being born time and time again. Indeed, this is probably one of the earliest of spiritual beliefs. Despite the growing evidence of the existence of past lives, there is not, and probably never will be any hard scientific proof for the existence of reincarnation. Indeed, it is arguable that stepping out from the need to have something proved, to a position of believing it is possible, to trusting it is probable, to knowing it is true, is a necessary step on the path of enlightenment.

If we can accept that in essence we are spiritual beings and not our physical bodies, and that our lives here on Earth are only transitory, then the existence of reincarnation and our own immortality becomes not just a possibility but arguably the only concept that really makes any sense. After all, if our three-score-and-ten years on Earth were all we had, why would anyone wish to do anything other than simply have a good time? Unless there's more than this, why should anyone wish to help ease the path of others?

What a relief this realisation can be! If we are born again, what is there to fear in death? As many ancient philosophies have taught for centuries, death is just a new beginning. Death is simply discarding our physical bodies and returning 'home' ready to start a new chapter. It can enable us to accept more readily the idea of our own physical demise as well as the death of loved ones.

The purpose of our life — indeed each of our lives — on Earth is to gain enlightenment. We do this through the experiences we have over many lifetimes. Each time we reincarnate, there is a new set of lessons to learn, new experiences to have. We choose the existence we will lead each lifetime, not down to the last detail but certainly the main building blocks of our lives that will best support us in learning the lessons we have set for ourselves. Details such as our parents, the time and place of our birth, our sexual orientation and physical characteristics, and our major relationships are not matters of chance but we have chosen for ourselves.

Reincarnation helps provide us with an answer as to why there should be what we often view as inequalities in the lives of different people, some with apparently undeserved misery and others with equally unmerited privileges. It could explain those feelings we all get from time to time of *déjà vu*. It might also answer the perennial question as to why God allows suffering and why so many people die such apparently meaningless deaths such as by murder, in wars, famines, floods, or by cot death. Perhaps the timing and manner of their death was part of the experiences they chose for themselves. Even if not, they have future lives to move on to.

Provided we learn the lessons we have come to learn, there is no need for us to repeat them; however, we will carry over the lessons from one lifetime to the next if they have not been learned the first time. We may in previous lives have been tyrants, bullies, killers — or worse! Each life, however, takes us further along the path of enlightenment. As we do so our need to control others becomes less and less. It can be helpful to realise, though, that whatever 'mistakes' we make in this life none is fatal. We can afford to make mistakes, although there is always a consequence for our actions and we may need to make amends, either in this or a future lifetime.

Once we realise we have lived on Earth before it can be quite natural to wonder what previous lives we have had, perhaps to wonder if we've been rich and famous or a beautiful princess, a great leader or some wealthy tzar. It is possible, through hypnotic regression, to visit past lives and re-live events from previous lifetimes, and this can be a fascinating subject to study. In most cases, whilst it may be of interest to know who we were or what we did in a previous lifetime, this is quite irrelevant to our present existence from the point of view of our spiritual development. For some people, however, it can be extremely helpful for them to know what has happened in previous lives to enable them heal some particular issue that has followed them unresolved from one lifetime to another. Care should always be taken to ensure that any regressions are carried out by a qualified practitioner.

## Example

The death of Diana, Princess of Wales, in August 1997 is an example of how energy operates in the world. The manner and timing of her death were a shock to many people, and there was a genuine sense of loss throughout many parts of the world, even by those who had little respect for her when she was alive. A lot of people were unable to explain the reason for their feelings. What is indisputable, though, is the real atmosphere of calm and peace that was created amidst the shock, the media hype and the desire to apportion blame. This is one of the most powerful demonstrations of the power of a collective conscious, how the feelings and thoughts of many people can become a shared experience and how it becomes amplified in the process.

Many people believe that despite her human failings she was an enlightened soul whose mission was to raise the consciousness of the planet — something she unquestionably achieved.

❖

# Self Esteem

The human condition for many of us at some stage of our lives or another is one of low — or at least lowered — self-esteem; of self-doubt, of not thinking ourselves good enough, and undervaluing not just ourselves, but also our accomplishments, our jobs, our qualities, our desires.

Low self-esteem can manifest itself in our lives in many different ways, some of which are not obvious; for example: lack of thought for others as well as self; always criticising other people; bullying; always deferring to others; always looking for the 'catch' when things are going well; demeaning our own achievements; always expecting 'the worst'; always accepting second-best; protecting ourselves from failure or disappointment; remaining in a job or a relationship that is past its 'sell-by' date; dependency on alcohol, drugs, sex or another person; failure to recognise the truth, preferring to believe our own version of what is real; etc., etc. Yes, it's a long list and I'm sure most of us can recognise ourselves in there somewhere!

There is nothing 'wrong' with someone who has low self-esteem. However, it can be a barrier to leading a fulfilling life here on Earth and is an obstacle to our spiritual development. It may be something we have had all of our lives. On the other hand, we may lose our sense of self-value as a result of some specific event, like being made redundant, or the breakdown of a relationship, or an accident.

When we have this condition, most of us are unaware of it to begin with, and would probably be offended and vehemently deny that we had low self-esteem were anyone to suggest as much. What is more, if challenged, we often try to justify our thoughts and actions by claiming we are just being realistic. Some people compensate for their low self-esteem by becoming aggressive, arrogant, bullying, inconsiderate, or what is often seen as over-confident. Others spend a large part of their lives accomplishing less than they are capable of, hiding away so as not to be noticed, flitting from one job to another or from one relationship to another, staying in a relationship that is not in their best interests, constantly talking themselves out of getting what they really want in life.

The first step to overcoming low self-esteem is to recognise that it's there, and acknowledge that it is not serving us. I repeat, there is nothing 'wrong', and we are not 'bad' people for having this condition. It can be comforting if we realise we're not alone in having this affliction; if we realise that society, our parents, our schooling, religion have all played their part in creating these circumstances. However, if we give in to it we deny an important part of who we really are; we create a life in which it is difficult if not impossible to fulfil our reason for being here on Earth in this lifetime, our *raison d'être*. We deny our spiritual nature. It is, therefore, an important step of our spiritual development to stop undermining ourselves and cultivate a healthy self-image.

Once we recognise that we *are* good enough, that we are loveable, worthy, perfect, whole, we find there is no need to continue trying to prove our superiority over others — or our inferiority to others. We know that in the sight of God everyone is special, although no one is better than anyone else; that we are all created equal, each with his or her own unique set of skills and talents. And if that's good enough for God, then it should be good enough for us! We can begin to learn to respect ourselves and others, and celebrate our differences as well as our similarities without prejududice.

Creating a positive self-image really is as simple as changing the way we think about ourselves, recognising when we are putting ourselves down, or talking ourselves out of something, and changing our thoughts to positive ones; ones which will help us achieve what we desire. It takes practice but it is possible and, as I mentioned already, it is an important stage on the path of enlightenment.

---

### Example

Mary was a successful woman. She had a first class honours degree and had worked her way up in her career to a good position in middle management. She was good at her work and was respected by her bosses, as well as her colleagues, and was often asked for her help. She had a good job, a pleasant home, a good circle of friends and as full a social life as she wanted. She considered herself to be reasonably self-confident and realistic.

However, Mary's confidence was sometimes little more than a veil, as she frequently undermined herself both in her own mind and to others – often in quite subtle ways. She allowed herself to be put upon by colleagues, often doing their work as well as her own. Whilst she wanted to be helpful, she had difficulty turning down requests for help even when it meant she had to take paperwork home in order to complete her own work, putting the needs of others above her own. Several of Mary's possessions were in a poor state, even though she could well afford to replace them or have them repaired. And when she did buy something she preferred to go to car-boot sales or second-hand shops rather than buy new, not because they were better quality items but because it was cheaper there. Subconsciously she felt she didn't deserve to have new things. She often told herself there was never enough time to do all the things she wanted to do, as though she didn't deserve to do everything. And Mary would brush off compliments and thanks, as though she didn't deserve them, which some people took as a snub.

It came as a shock to Mary to find she had low self-esteem. However, once she overcame her initial sense of disbelief, guilt and recriminations, she began to understand the value of re-building her self-confidence and self-image. She found that just by recognising the fact, she was able to see when she was putting herself down and could find alternative ways of dealing with the situation. As she did so she found the quality of her life changed considerably for the better. She found alternative ways to assist her colleagues and bosses at work without doing their work for them, which won her greater respect and gave her more leisure time. By not hanging onto possessions she no longer used and repairing or replacing things that were broken, she found a new sense of her own value, an appreciation for her belongings and an unwillingness always to make do with second best.

### Exercise

Now's the time to be honest with yourself! Find a quiet spot, play some classical music if you wish, and perhaps light a candle. Sit comfortably and relax your body and your mind. Take a few deep breaths, holding your breath for a few seconds each time before exhaling. Allow your body and your mind to get into a deeper state of relaxation with each breath, and then open your notebook.

Write down as many ways as you can think of in which you frequently, or occasionally, undermine yourself. Take your time and remember you're only short-changing yourself if you are not being completely honest. There are no 'right' or 'wrong' answers, just those that are true for you.

List all those nagging doubts you have from time to time, however subtle; the thoughts that keep you from achieving your dreams; the 'stories' you tell yourself to justify when you don't quite finish those things you intended to do; how you react to 'bad' news, criticism, unexpected events; how you react to the idea of trying something new; the things you tell yourself you 'can't' do; the things you tell yourself you don't deserve, or that you're being selfish in wanting.

When you've finished, review the list. Commit it to memory so you can recognise when you are talking or thinking yourself small. Resolve to change your negative programming. Then in your daily life learn to recognise when you are undermining yourself and simply change the messages you give yourself to ones that will encourage rather than discourage you. It takes practice, but you can learn to catch your thoughts and change them. Keep at it!

It is worth coming back to this list from time to time, reviewing it and adding to it — and deleting those traits and conversations you have successfully re-programmed — so you are aware of the ways in which you act and react and how you are making progress. It is only when we are aware of ourselves that we can change.

❖

# Change

It would probably be an understatement to say that we do not always find change comfortable or easy. Many of us — individuals, corporations, governments — fiercely resist any suggestion of change. It can appear threatening. We will go to extraordinary lengths to avoid change, denying that there is any need for it, or claiming that the 'fault' lies elsewhere, that someone or something else must change, but not us. Or we will tinker around the edges of a question rather than address the real issue. We will invent completely spurious arguments to support us in maintaining the *status quo*. The simple truth is that we are frightened of change.

However, change is an inevitable part of life. It is as inescapable as death. Change is essential for the growth of us all as individuals, for the evolution of humankind and for the unfolding of the entire universe. If we can accept this premise then it will make our lives so much smoother, for whenever we resist something — even something as apparently simple as change — we give that something incredible power. And the more we resist, the greater the power it assumes and the less power we have over it. As a simple example, the more we push against a closed door, the more difficult it becomes to open it.

Even if the issue is one that would be of obvious benefit to whole sections of society or to the whole of humankind, such as world peace, there are always those who will resist the changes that are needed to bring it about. For a start, there are the army leaders and those in the arms trade whose *raison d'être* would be virtually eliminated were we to attain world peace. There are also many politicians and individuals who peddle discord, aggression, mistrust or outright hostility. For them, too, the mere idea of world peace is a threat.

Understanding that resistance to change comes from our fears can enable us to put things into perspective. This can help us deal with other people's apparent unwillingness to change and learn to overcome our own resistance.

### Example

Ever since he graduated from college and started his first job, Alan wished he would be able to work for himself one day. He would mention his ambition of being his own boss at every opportunity to colleagues and friends. However, being in a well-paid job, he was too comfortable and secure to make the jump from being employed to becoming self-employed.

Then, after fifteen years, his employer was taken over and Alan found himself threatened with redundancy. He and his other colleagues in the same situation immediately started scouring the newspaper jobs columns for possible positions. In the process of doing so he also spoke with several of his former colleagues, one of whom asked him if he had been serious about starting his own business, as he might have six months work for him. Well, Alan was over the moon! Following a couple of interviews he was offered a six-month contract, which was later extended to a year, and in that time Alan started finding himself other clients.

He felt the universe had given him the kick up the backside he needed to get himself on the self-employment trail. 'You've talked of working for yourself for long enough,' it seemed to say. 'Now's the time to stop talking and get on with it!'

### Exercise

Find yourself a place where you can be in peace. Play some background music and light a candle if you wish. Sit comfortably and take a deep breath; breathe in as far as you can, filling your lungs with air. Hold your breath for a few seconds and then breathe out, allowing all the tension to flow out of your body as you exhale. Let go of any thoughts you might have. Take several more deep breaths and each time feel your body and your mind relax further. Become aware of your steady breathing.

Now take your notebook. Think of something you have long wanted to do. Write it down. Next, list all the things that stop you achieving this goal. What needs to change? What are your fears? What stories do you tell yourself to keep you from this aim? What are your justifications? How would you feel if you did achieve your goal? Take about twenty minutes to write down whatever comes to you; try not to think too hard. When you have finished, review your list. What does this tell you about your fears? About yourself? About your desires?

You may want to share anything you have learned with your companion or buddy if you have one. Whatever else, make sure you write in your notebook what you have discovered about yourself.

❖

# The Present

Living in the present, in the here and now, sounds like such a straightforward and desirable principle. The trouble is most of us spend much of our time living either in the past or in the future.

There is nothing 'wrong' in looking forward — to our holiday, our next date, payday, the end of our journey, or whatever, nor in making plans for the future. However, if we spend too much time looking towards the future we run the risk of missing what is going on in the present moment. We suddenly find on coming back to the present that we have been on 'automatic pilot' and have a blank recollection of whatever has recently happened.

Equally — and more prevalent — is that we spend much of our time in the past. Even when we are not actually reliving or reminiscing or worrying about the past, or fighting for yesterday's dreams, we often interpret current events or anticipate future events in the light of our past experiences. We expect people to react in the same ways as they have before, or in the same ways we would react, or in the ways we have been taught that they 'should' react. And we have similar expectations about places and events. In doing so we not only limit ourselves and our possible experience of the situation but we also devalue the other people involved.

There is a fine line between learning from past successes and 'mistakes', and living in the past. It is important to recognise that it is our past that has brought us to where we are right now in our lives. The lessons, experiences, relationships, deeds and misdeeds we have had and done all go to make up who we are now. We may need to learn to accept and reconcile some aspects of our past, understanding what lessons there were for us in the situation and possibly forgiving ourselves or others for any perceived transgressions. Having done so we are free to move on.

Every moment is an opportunity to create a new reality irrespective of what has happened in the past. The key is not to *re*-act to situations — because re-acting is always based on the past — but to *act* without any preconceptions of what might or might not occur and allow ourselves to have a completely new experience rather than repeating the same experience time and time again.

When we are not living in the moment (the present), we are elsewhere (not present). It is no coincidence that the same word has these two very slightly different connotations.

## Example

Doug had been fighting to save the law school he had founded when he suffered a massive heart attack. The law school was a unique, one-of-a-kind establishment dedicated to social justice, and it was facing closure. As he was to learn later, his heart attack was so severe that his consultant admitted he had never known anyone survive from such damage. It slowly dawned on Doug that he had to abandon the fight for his beloved law school and start fighting for his own life! He realised the law school was yesterday's fight and that he had to let go. He needed to focus on his own health right now. In time he recovered and he went on to do other social justice work.

## Exercise

Take yourself off to your quiet space. Light a candle and play some background music if this appeals to you. Sit quietly and allow all thoughts to vanish from your mind. Take a deep breath. Breathe in fully and hold your breath for several seconds; breathe out. Repeat this three or four times, each time allowing both your body and your mind to find a deeper state of relaxation.

With your notebook to hand think about what you might be holding onto from the past. They might be possessions, keepsakes, plants, friendships, thoughts, memories, opinions. Make a list of as many as you can without prejudging them in any way. Just write them down. Then take each item on your list and examine it; consider whether or not it is 'past its sell-by date'. For each item that seems to have had its day, release it. Let it go with love. You may wish to say a few simple words, such as "[item] I lovingly release you and wish you well on the rest of your journey". Alternatively, you may wish to write a letter or a note on tissue paper saying what the item meant to you and saying that you release it. When you have finished, reread the note and then flush it down the toilet. If the item is something physical be sure to dispose of it in a suitable manner.

With your special friend you may wish to share anything that particularly struck you during this process.

❖

# Love

'God is love'; 'Love makes the world go round'; 'Love conquers all'. There are many sayings in everyday use about the importance of love. They're all true, but how often do we simply recite them without really understanding them? The simple truth is that love is the energy that keeps the world running. Love keeps our hearts beating; it maintains our landscape, the hills, the rivers and the mountains; it ensures the reproduction of plants and animals; it is an energy of attraction. And no, I'm not suggesting that sex and love are the same thing! The importance of cultivating love in every department of our lives cannot be understated. I'm not talking about sentimental love here, although that has its place. Nor is it to do with conditional love, the kind that depends on our moods or the actions of ourselves or other people in order to gain their acceptance of us, or for us to accept them. It is about unconditional love, or divine love.

This has to begin with ourselves. Unless we love ourselves we cannot truly love anyone else, and we cannot accept the love that someone else may have for us. The Bible exhorts us to 'love your neighbour as yourself' (Leviticus 19:18), but this presupposes that we love ourselves. For many of us this is not something that comes naturally or easily. Guilt, low self-esteem, judgement of ourselves and others, lack of forgiveness, wishing things were different from the way they are all show that self-love is missing. Unconditional love means just that — loving ourselves and others without condition, accepting them just the way they are with all their perceived imperfections, without demanding they do this, that or the other to earn or love; just as God — or the universe — accepts us the way we are.

The only way we can receive love is to give love, and the only way we have any love to give to someone else is if we first have love for ourselves. Anything else is an illusion. Sometimes we kid ourselves that we love someone else when in fact we are simply taking the love they have for us, creating a dependence on them and draining them, giving nothing back.

If we're not coming from a position of unconditional love, then we're acting out of fear. There is only love or fear, and if our love is conditional on something being received then it is simply fear by another name. We all have our insecurities. It is just that some of us have more than others and some of us allow our insecurities to keep us back in life more than others. When we withhold ourselves in case we get hurt, when we change our behaviour as the result of someone else's actions or words, when we love someone only so long as they love us in return, we can be sure that fear is at work. Fear keeps us in the past, worrying that we will repeat past 'mistakes'. On the other hand, love enables us to experience new joys and new heights of happiness. Yes, love requires us to take risks. But the converse of this is that unless we're prepared to take risks we will never experience true unconditional love.

Cultivating unconditional love is part of the journey of enlightenment for all who are on that path.

We can help to create a life filled with unconditional love by learning to be thankful for everything we have and everything that happens in our lives. It is always easy to be grateful when things are going well for us, but even so, how often do we say 'thank you' to the universe for the 'good things'? More difficult, but equally important, is to learn to be thankful for the unpleasant things in life, for upsets to our plans, for bills that are higher than expected, for those people we find most trying, for unrequited love.

We can learn to be thankful for everything in our lives once we recognise that they provide opportunities for growth and learning. For Monday mornings, for rainy days, unexpected bills, awkward customers, accidents, that cycle tyre puncture and that bruised shin, as well as all the pleasurable things we find it easy to be thankful for. Even if we do not see it at the time, there is a silver lining in every cloud.

### Example

With a slim income Janet had a very simple life and whenever an unexpected expense arrived, such as home repairs or new clothes for her young daughter, it always threw her into confusion and was met with curses and complaints as to how she was 'expected' to find the money to pay the bill. She hated having to get up early on Monday mornings after a weekend of staying in bed till midday. And she also found it difficult to keep boyfriends, always finding something about them she didn't agree with.

When she first heard about the need to be thankful for everything in her life, Janet scoffed. 'Be thankful for never having enough money?' she moaned. 'And all the guys I meet that are more trouble than they're worth!' Months later, still struggling to juggle her finances, and after the end of another 'disastrous' short relationship, she eventually conceded there would be nothing to lose by giving it a try. So every night in bed she would run through her day saying 'thank you' for everything that occurred during her day. She found it easy to say 'thanks' for the things that had gone the way she had hoped and in a funny way it felt sort-of 'right'. However, Janet found it difficult to say 'thanks' for the things she didn't really appreciate; but she persevered and said 'thank you' for the opportunities they presented her with and the lessons they opened for her to learn, even if she didn't yet know what those opportunities and lessons were.

As she continued with this practice night after night she found it became easier to thank the universe for everything in her life; she began to see the lessons she was being given the opportunity to learn, and somehow all of her life became a lot easier. However, she asked that her lessons should not be revealed here in case it should detract from your own lessons.

### Exercise

Each night when you go to bed, take time to go over everything that has happened during the day. Without judging anything as 'good' or 'bad' simply list them one by one, saying 'thank you' to the universe, or to your God, for them all. Remember that some events may have been a blessing in disguise. Ask for guidance in learning the lessons that those things you had difficulty with were there to teach you. As this becomes part of your regular routine you will find that thankfulness becomes second nature, that you begin to recognise that there is a purposefulness in everything that happens in your life. Doing this before you go to sleep helps you to finish the day in a positive, thankful frame of mind.

After a week or two of following this exercise each night you might wish to make some notes in your notebook about what you have learned, and/or you may share with your buddy or special friend.

❖

# Responsibility

The principle of responsibility is one of the main tenets of spirituality (or enlightenment). In everyday usage, 'responsibility' usually equates to 'blame'. However, in the context of spiritual awareness there is no concept of blame, no 'right' or 'wrong' — simply what is. That is not to say there are no consequences for our actions (and our thoughts). On the contrary, every action, every inaction and every thought has its consequence; the consequence may be benign or it may not be so favourable, the extent of the consequence may be limited or it may be far reaching, but there is always a consequence.

Responsibility is not something we accept (or perhaps do not accept), or that we assume or take, or give to someone else. It is simply there. And the consequences of our actions, our inactions and our thoughts will occur regardless of whether or not we 'accept' or recognise our responsibilities.

The thing is, we are responsible for everything that happens in our lives. Everything that occurs in our lives is the result of some previous thought, action, or inaction. It may have been minutes earlier, days, weeks or years ago, or even in a previous lifetime.

Starting even before our birth, we choose the place and time of our birth, our nationality, our personal characteristics and the experiences we wish to work through and the lessons we wish to learn during this lifetime, as well as many of the people who will help us work through these experiences, including our parents. Everyone that comes into our lives does so, not by accident or coincidence, but because we have invited them for a reason. Quite often that reason is to help us to 'learn' a particular lesson or work through a specific experience, and it is often those with whom we have most difficulty that are the greatest help to us, even if it doesn't seem that way at the time.

To help us better understand responsibility, we need to shed the idea of things as being 'good' or 'bad', or 'right' or 'wrong', and of blaming others for the circumstances in which we find ourselves. We need to drop the idea that when something works out differently from the way we had intended or wanted that we've somehow 'failed'. Simply changing our perspective can help to bring new insights to events that occur during our life.

Once we understand that we are not our bodies, our thoughts, our feelings, or the sum total of these, that we are not human beings having a spiritual experience but spiritual beings having a human experience, then we can begin to see our lives from a spiritual rather than a human perspective. It helps us to see that everything that happens to us in this lifetime — indeed our entire life itself — is just a passing phase.

This is not to say that we should take lightly crimes against humanity; or crimes against the person, such as rape, mugging, torture, murder and the like; or disasters such as aeroplane crashes, volcanoes, floods and hurricanes; or even crimes against property. It does not mean we should ignore them or that crimes should go unpunished. Nor does it mean we should ignore the plight of the homeless, or refugees, or turn a blind eye to others in need. On the contrary, it means we have a responsibility to treat all those concerned with compassion and understanding, and that we should do whatever we can to assist them in whatever way we are best placed to help. However, it does enable us to take a different view of life, to see the bigger picture. Even death is not the end, simply 'returning home', the start of a new phase of our life.

It is also the case that trauma and adversity can lead to growth and learning. Every experience offers that opportunity, and quite often the more traumatic the experience the more profound the lesson and the greater the potential for a shift in attitudes. There are many people who, having undergone extreme experiences such as losing loved ones in tragic circumstances, have then dedicated their lives to helping others going through the same experience, or helping to find a cure for little-known illnesses, or supporting the bereaved. It is our interpretation of the events in our lives and how we react to them that determines whether we grow spiritually or whether we stay where we are.

Then again, we are all responsible for the state of our own country, our society, our world and our environment. It is no good us blaming politicians or other nations, for that is not the way of the spiritually responsible. Whether or not we exercise our right to vote — those of us who live in a democratic society — we elect our politicians.

Another aspect of personal responsibility is the recognition that each one of us is on this Earth at this time for a specific purpose. We are not here by accident or on a whim. We are all here to serve humankind in some way. It is not for someone else to tell us what that purpose is. We already know, we just need to remember what it is. What is clear, though, is that none of us is called upon to 'play small' or to hide away. We are called to be the greatest we are capable of. Nothing less! As Nelson Mandela said in his inaugural speech in 1994, 'We were born to make manifest the glory of God that is within us.'

Scary? Of course, you could choose to see it that way! But then you could also choose to see it as exciting, as an opportunity to make a difference in the world — not for any selfish or egotistical reasons, or any sense of 'what's in it for me', but simply from a desire to be of service in humility with an understanding that this is what you came here to do.

### Example

One morning John was walking his dog when he came across a bottle lying on the pavement. Perhaps he thinks about picking up the bottle and disposing of it carefully, but he doesn't do so. Then, the following morning, he finds the bottle has been broken, and his dog cuts her paw on the broken glass. John is responsible for the injury to his dog. He could have done something to prevent it, but failed to do so. It doesn't make him 'bad' or 'wrong', it simply means there was a consequence of his inaction; in this case it was injury to his dog. It is something he could have avoided but he chose not to.

It doesn't mean he should go round picking up every bottle he finds on the street — of course, he may choose to do so, to ensure his dog does not cut her paw again, or as a public service. Either way he has a choice, and depending on his choice there will be one of several consequences. Nor does it mean that the person who left the bottle on the pavement in the first place or the person who smashed it are not responsible for their actions — they are equally responsible and will each experience some consequence of their action. However, each of us is only responsible for our own responsibility!

### Exercise

Find a spot to be quiet and comfortable; put on some background music if you wish. Take a few deep breaths; breathe in as far as you can; fill your lungs; hold your breath for a few seconds; then breathe in some more; exhale. Repeat this two or three more times feeling your body relax further with each breath.

Think back to a situation where something got damaged or broken, or where someone was hurt or something was lost, where your first instinct was to blame someone else for what occurred. Recall the situation as it happened. In your notebook write down the situation and how you saw it and why you considered the other person to be at fault. What were your thoughts and feelings before and after the situation?

Again, take a few deep breaths. Then take a look at the situation from the position of responsibility. See how it looks and feels different. Consider whether you may have contributed to the result in some way or what you might have done differently. This might be difficult to begin with. Just keep at it. Do not censor your thoughts; write down anything that comes to mind. When you have finished write down what thoughts and insights come to you.

If you wish, you may compare notes with your companion on this course if you have one.

You may wish to repeat this exercise with other situations, either now or at a later time.

❖

# Integrity

Integrity has to do with being consistent, or whole. It is about being true to our values. To use management-speak, it is about 'walking our talk'; that is, saying, thinking and acting consistently. When we say one thing and do another we are out of integrity with ourselves; we are being inconsistent.

This is not so much about the particular values we hold, as simply whether or not we are true to them. And it has nothing to do with moral judgement, about being 'right' or 'wrong'. Indeed, one of the most integrous people of the twentieth century was Adolph Hitler. Whether or not you admire the man — and the chances are since you're reading this book that you do not! — is not the point. The thing is that his actions were entirely consistent with his words; he walked and talked hatred, murder and fear. But enough of that!

As with all matters of judgement, we must guard against measuring other people against our own set of values. Just because our own values include, say, honesty and truthfulness this does not mean these will be the values of others. And it does not suggest that someone who acts without honesty or truth is necessarily out of integrity.

It is only when we are in integrity that we can hope to achieve our aims, whatever they are. If we say one thing and do another we are giving conflicting messages to the universe about what we actually want. The result is at best stalemate or confusion, and there will be little or no progress towards our aims whilst we remain out of integrity with ourselves.

This principle applies not just to our lives as a whole but also to each and every department of our lives and to individual events. Whilst we can be in integrity in some areas of our lives but out of integrity in other departments, the overall result in our life is imbalance. For some people, perhaps, their job can be inconsistent with the rest of their lives. This can lead to stress or strained relationships or feelings that something 'isn't quite right'. When we live our lives in integrity we find that we are at peace with ourselves and with those with whom we share our lives on a personal level as well as at work.

## Example

Pierre had experienced a number of set-backs in his life, all of which he had won through and which, looking back after the event, he realised had helped to make him a stronger person. He decided to write a book passing on the learnings he had gleaned that had helped him through some of the toughest periods of his life. His book was a masterpiece, and he found someone willing to publish it. However, it was very slow in selling. Despite its charm and obvious conviction, the book simply did not move.

At the same time, Pierre was complaining about all his debts and one or two significant people in his life who he blamed for the state of his life. He was clearly a man of integrity in his everyday life and had written his book with a genuine wish to be of help to others. However, there was a distinct lack of consistency in what his book talked about and what he was saying, both to himself and his friends.

Although he adamantly affirmed his integrity was intact, he continued to be a victim of his circumstances. Only once he worked through his feelings and accepted responsibility for the people in his life did Pierre's book start to sell. It took him several months to work through. It was not an easy process for him as there were a lot of buried emotions, and he had to face up to a few (what he considered to be) unpalatable truths. However, with each step in his personal quest he made strides with his book, which eventually became a best seller.

### Exercise

Find a place to get comfortable. Play some soft music and light a candle if this helps. Relax. Take a few deep breaths. Breathe in deeply, hold your breath for a few seconds and then breathe out. Repeat this three or four times, each time allowing your body and your mind to become more relaxed.

Take your notebook and note down past situations where there have been inconsistencies in one or more compartments of your life. At this point it would be easier to consider past events or circumstances rather than present ones; you can come back to those later. Do this without judging yourself or the situation as 'bad' or 'wrong'. If you cannot immediately find examples of inconsistency, look to see where the results you have achieved in some area of your life have differed from what you wanted or what you thought you wanted. Then look for the inconsistencies.

Now consider in what area the contradiction lay and what would need to be different to bring the situation into integrity. Write down what ideas come to you. Take your time, and allow your heart rather than your mind to speak to you.

If you are working with a friend or buddy you may wish to share what you have learned in this exercise, if not the precise circumstances.

You may wish to repeat this exercise either now or later, perhaps when you have finished the book, with present circumstances where there are inconsistencies in your life. Consider what might be changed to bring about a more consistent, peaceful existence.

❖

# Judgement

Most of us are faced with judgement daily in various areas of our lives. Some of us judge — or are judged by — our partners, our children, our parents, our work colleagues, our friends, our political leaders, those in the news, and even complete strangers. We judge other people, others judge us and we judge ourselves, in various circumstances, as 'good' or 'bad', 'right' or 'wrong'. Some of the world's major religions even teach us that God judges us, too, and that as a result of his judgement we shall either be admitted to heaven or condemned to hell for ever.

When you see someone in the street, what is your first thought about that person? Is it, 'Isn't he fat!', or, 'She's pretty', or whatever? Do you notice first a person's physical appearance, the colour of their skin, their size and shape, or what they're wearing? Or do you think, 'There goes another child of God'?

Do you find yourself thinking about the 'right' or 'wrong' of other people's actions — in the news, on the road, while you're going about your day, or in conversations with others? Do you find yourself telling other people, or yourself, what they 'ought' to do in a particular circumstance. All these can be indications of how judgemental you are in your everyday life.

Perhaps it's not all that surprising given the amount of negative 'programming' we all receive as children; the attention given by the media to all that is 'wrong' in the world; the adversarial nature of our political and legal systems, which are intent on proving one side 'right' at the expense of the other; and religious teachings. Our society seems obsessed with how we appear to others and the aim of much modern advertising is to make us feel inadequate so we will buy the advertised products to fill this perceived deficiency in our lives.

But then judgement is not just about negative thoughts and feelings — although our negative judgements do generally tend to outweigh the positive ones. We also find ourselves approving of the actions of others or considering their actions to be 'good' or 'right'. What is important to remember is that judgement, whether positive or negative, is unhelpful and in some sense limiting the other person, as well as limiting ourselves in our spiritual quest. I don't mean that we should not encourage others or express our opinions, but that they should be done with respect, without judgement, and without trying to impose our views on other people.

When we judge others or compare ourselves with others, whether favourably or not, we are judging not just the other person but also ourselves. We see in others a reflection of ourselves. When we 'approve' of someone else it is because we see in that person some aspect of ourselves that we like. When we 'disapprove' of someone else we are expressing our dissatisfaction with some aspect of our own lives or with our circumstances.

Contrary to what we are often taught, the universe — or God, if you prefer — doesn't judge us. Why then should we judge ourselves, or each other? What a relief it is for many of us to learn that we don't always have to be 'right' and forever be looking for things that need to be fixed. Acceptance of 'what is' is one of the keys to inner peace.

Just as there are no 'right' or 'wrong', 'good' or 'bad' events in our lives, so too there are no 'good', 'bad', 'right' or 'wrong' people, just other spiritual beings working through their human experiences on Earth.

So why not let us learn to cultivate respect for others; for views and opinions that differ from our own; for people whose values and morals are not the same as our own? Perhaps in the process there are things we can learn from others. Acceptance of life, and of other people just the way they are is one of the keys to enlightenment, to peace, spiritual understanding and inner calm. We don't have to agree with other people's views or actions, simply accept them as part of some other being's truth.

When we catch ourselves thinking of someone judgementally, we can counter those negative energies by wishing the person well, by mentally blessing them. Indeed, it can be good practice to bless the people we come into contact with each day, especially those we find arrogant or aggressive or just plain difficult. Spreading love is one of the most effective ways in which we can bring a positive influence to our surroundings, and transform what might have been a negative situation into one of positive influences.

### Example

Jane was, on the whole, a considerate car driver. However, she used to find she was always critical of drivers who were not as courteous as herself. Everywhere she went, whether as a driver or passenger in a car, on foot or on her cycle, she would notice cars or vans parked on the pavements, drivers that ignored people waiting at pedestrian crossings trying to cross the road, drivers that cut in front of another car causing them to brake or swerve, that followed too closely behind the car in front, that ran traffic lights. The examples she found were legion. Jane seethed inwardly, not wanting to create conflict by confronting the drivers concerned. She knew it was raising her stress levels, and that her becoming stressed was doing nothing to improving the driving of others. Eventually she realised that if she wasn't going to change other people by becoming agitated there was only one thing to do — *change her attitude!*

Jane figured that if she stopped viewing everyone else as 'wrong', inconsiderate and arrogant, even if it didn't change their driving, it would mean she would have a less stressful experience, and she would not be passing on her frustrations to her passengers and possibly to other road users. So each time she started a journey, however short, before starting the engine she closed her eyes, took several deep breaths and pictured a calm and stress-free driving experience. Whenever another driver performed some inconsiderate manoeuver she quietly whispered 'bless you' to them. Jane was surprised at the difference it made to her journeys. Not only did she find the whole experience less stressful, but she also came to realise there were fewer 'bad' drivers than she seemed to experience before. She was delighted and resolved to try the same techniques in other situations where she was being judgemental about others.

### Exercise

Take yourself to somewhere quite. Sit comfortably and put on some music if you wish and perhaps light a candle. Take a few deep breaths; breathe in deeply, hold your breath for a few seconds, then breathe out. Feel your body relax with each breath. Let all thoughts out of your mind and relax your mind, too.

Think of an example of when you think of other people as 'wrong', selfish, inconsiderate, impossible. Hint: it is usually when you find your stress-levels rising. Write down in your notebook what most niggles you about these situations and the people involved. How do you feel? How do you react to them? How do you think they feel? How do you want them to be different? How would you feel if they were different? How might you change your attitude to the situation so as not to become stressed and angry or frustrated? How would it feel not to be stressed? What would be the effect on those around you? What would you need to do to make this part of your regular way of life? What effect does this have on other areas of your life and on other people in your life? Write down in your notebook your answers to these questions and whatever else comes to you.

When you have finished, but not before, if you are working with someone else you may wish to compare notes.

❖

# Relationships

For many of us relationships are one of the main ways in which we learn about ourselves and about life. Relationships are a way of reflecting back things about ourselves that we need to know in order to grow. Very often we are not aware of the messages we are receiving. Nor are we aware that we invite these people into our lives. Indeed, until we recognise the message, or at least learn the lesson it is there to teach us, we will continue to attract the same kind of people until we finally take notice.

Perhaps it is hard for us to accept that we invite people into our lives at all, and to understand that they are there to help us. We may often complain that we don't want people like this in our lives, that there is something wrong with them. However, once we accept that we are at essence spiritual beings, that we are here to learn through our experiences and our interaction with others, then we will begin to take full responsibility for our relationships and all that goes on within them.

For all of us it is our parents with whom we have our first and usually our most enduring relationships, and this is true even for those who have been orphaned or abandoned by one or both of our parents. It is with them that we often have most to learn, and perhaps to teach, which is why many of us often have so many 'issues' with our parents. Whether it is lessons around abandonment, control, abuse, co-dependency, anger, poverty or whatever, for many of us it can take the best part of our lifetime to work through some of the issues our parents are here to help us with. And we are here to help our parents with their own lessons, for all relationships are two-way affairs.

Similarly, all our key relationships, whether in our personal or business lives, are there to help us learn important lessons, and the people who come into our lives to help us with these lessons do so at our invitation. They therefore deserve our most grateful thanks for heeding our subconscious calls for support, even though more often than not they receive curses, if not outwardly expressed then at least inwardly.

When we feel there is something 'wrong' or missing within a relationship this is usually an indication of something amiss within ourselves. For all we ever see in someone else is a reflection of some aspect of ourselves; we can only recognise a trait that is part of our own make-up. Once we realise this, we start to look on relationships differently. When we meet someone with whom we have difficulty or if we run into difficulty within a relationship, we can ask ourselves what that person is there to help us learn.

### Example

Jenny found she was always attracting men and boyfriends who seemed to belittle her or verbally abuse her. They were never physically abusive, but she found the verbal attacks just as hurtful, perhaps more so.

It started with her father, who was always telling her she'd never make much of her life. She left home when she was nineteen to marry her school sweetheart, Sam, who was two years older than her. Jenny soon found Sam was so much like her father that she wondered how she never noticed this before they married. The sense of worthlessness that Jenny felt had led to her putting on weight and she took little interest in her appearance. Sam would go out every evening with his mates insisting that Jenny stayed at home, other than at weekends when she visited her parents while Sam went to watch football or the pub with his pals. He told her he was ashamed to be seen with her. When she failed to become pregnant her sense of worthlessness only got worse, and

Jenny suspected Sam was having an affair with a woman he met in the pub.

After three years Jenny and Sam got divorced. Jenny immediately moved in with another man who she soon found out was worse than both Sam and her father. She stayed with him for six tormenting months before getting a flat on her own. Over the next few years Jenny had a series of 'disastrous' affairs which all managed to confirm her poor opinion of herself. Finally she decided that she would be better off living on her own.

Then after a few years on her own she met David who seemed so different from all the others, someone who seemed to see beneath the facade of self-doubt and self-deprecation to what he called 'the real Jenny'. Having by now had enough of the verbal abuse, humiliation and self-hatred Jenny was ready to hear a different story. She found it hard to believe that David really liked her for what she was; she thought there was some hidden motive; she kept expecting him to start criticising her. But she seemed ready to give it a go; she found his attention and affection endearing. Slowly she began to believe that perhaps she was lovable and deserving and 'okay', and she found she was losing some weight without even trying. She took an interest in her appearance and David bought her some pretty clothes. She felt more healthy, more alive, more appreciative of the things in her life — especially David.

Jenny started, painfully at first, to look back at the unhappy times and began to see what they had taught her. For reasons she didn't understand, these people — her father, her first husband and her several boyfriends had been necessary to teach her to value herself as a woman and as a human being. In some way perhaps they were necessary for her to understand that there was something different.

### Exercise

Find somewhere quiet and relaxing. Play some soft music and light a candle if you feel like doing so. Close your eyes and take a deep breath; hold your breath for a few moments and then breathe out slowly feeling you body relax as you do so. Repeat this a further three or four times (or more), allowing your body to relax further each time. Relax your mind and let go of any thoughts.

Take your notebook and think of one of the relationships you have had that has given you a lot to handle, one with which you had a certain amount of difficulty. It needn't be the most difficult relationship you have had and it may have been with a friend, a lover, your parents, a boss or colleague at work, a neighbour or indeed anyone. It may be a recent or a long-past relationship, but it should be one that has finished rather than a current relationship.

Think about what it was about the relationship or the other person that gave you most difficulty. How did you behave towards them? How did you react to them? What similarities, if any, were there between this relationship and others you've had? What has it (or have they) had to teach you? Have you learned the lessons, or do you need other experiences to fully take in the lessons it had to teach you?

You may wish to share any particular insights you gained during this exercise with your special friend or companion.

You may find it useful to repeat this exercise with other relationships. In particular, it can be an extremely useful exercise to do when you have difficulties within an existing relationship.

❖

# Giving and Receiving

The Bible teaches us that it is more blessed to give than to receive (Acts 20:35). But note that it says *more* blessed; it does not say that it is not blessed to receive; it does not say we should not receive or we should not be open to receiving. It is still blessed to receive, just *more* blessed to give. I believe this is important.

Receiving should not be confused with taking; the two are quite different. Receiving is the acceptance of something offered freely by another person. Taking something that has not been offered is not the same thing at all.

Giving does not necessarily mean spending a lot of money, although of course it might do. As well as gifts for birthdays, anniversaries or other celebrations, we might give a smile, a compliment, an offer of help, a lift in the car, our time. A gift that comes from the heart is always more valuable than one that is of purely monetary value.

Many of us have great difficulty in receiving things. Perhaps we have learnt that is it 'wrong' or 'impolite' to accept something even when it is offered. Or maybe we feel that somehow we don't deserve it, or we're embarrassed to accept, or we feel we would be 'in debt' to the other person by accepting. These are selfish, ego-driven reasons. We may need to examine our motives and learn to accept gifts, compliments or assistance more readily when they are offered, and do so with gratitude and humility and love. Of course, there will be times when we feel we should decline something. If we are clear about our motives then we will know when it is in the best interests of all concerned to accept or decline.

Perhaps some of us need to learn to give and receive from ourselves — time off for pleasure, treats from time to time, rest — although in doing so we may need to guard against over-indulgence.

We must remember that it is only by receiving that we allow another person to give. If we refuse to receive what is offered, or if we accept it grudgingly with a dismissive word or manner, then we are denying the person an opportunity to give. We are in reality taking from the other person and we may be in danger of contributing to that person feeling worthless, that they have nothing worthwhile to give.

It is important for us to find a balance in our giving and receiving. We need to guard against denying someone the opportunity of giving to us by always giving to them. And if we are always receiving without giving anything in return then here too there is an imbalance.

### Example

A group of young people from a volunteer group had arranged to do some gardening for a pensioner whose garden had become a little too much for her. The volunteers duly arrived with their gardening tools, their youthful enthusiasm and their energy, and they were eagerly received by the elderly lady. The youngsters set to work and soon had piles of weeds and cuttings.

The lady was delighted with the help as well as the company and asked them what they would all like to drink. One of the youngsters jumped up and, waving aside all the old lady's protestations, went to make all the drinks for the team and the old lady. When the drinks arrived they all sat down and one or two of the volunteers chatted to the old lady. Eventually, the job was finished. The volunteers put all their cuttings and weeds into black bags and left them for collection with the rubbish.

As they left the lady sighed. How much she wished that they had allowed her to make the tea — just to do something, however small, in return. Somehow she felt rather superfluous and helpless. Oh, she was grateful for their help and the company, but it did seem to take away something from the value of their gift that she had not been permitted to give something back.

## Exercise

One interesting and rewarding way to experience being of service to others is to practise random acts of kindness or give anonymously knowing the recipient will be unaware of who it was that made a difference to their day, or why. For example, you may wish to send an anonymous postal order to an animal or children's charity; visit a hospital and spend some time chatting with someone who seldom receives any visitors, perhaps taking them a small bunch of flowers (the hospital receptionist will usually be delighted to direct you to a suitable ward if you explain your quest). You could pay a compliment to a complete stranger — without getting overly personal, which could seem threatening to some vulnerable people — you might complement them on part of their clothing or their hair or smile. Or you could let the person behind you in the supermarket queue go first, or help an elderly person to carry their shopping home, or pay the toll for the car behind on a toll bridge or ferry. Even just smiling at someone or saying 'hello' can make a big difference.

Consider the above examples and add some more of your own if you like. Make a commitment to perform some act of generosity every day for a period of, say, one month. Notice what difference it makes to the other person, and how you feel, too. Be prepared to have some of your offers of help rejected outright or to be met with suspicion. That is part of the process; many people are distrustful of the motives of anyone offering help. If your motives are genuine you will rise above other people's suspicions.

Share what you have learned through this exercise with your companion or buddy if you feel so inclined.

❖

# Abundance

The natural state of the universe is one of abundance. There is plenty of love, food, wealth, time, creative energy, success, etc. to go round. More than enough for everyone, for all our needs. Like love, abundance relies on there being a free flow of energy in order to flourish. If we block that flow then we make it difficult for ourselves to recognise and accept the abundance that is all around us.

It is our fears of there not being enough or that we don't deserve to have enough — our poverty-consciousness — that creates shortages. Our fears of shortage lead us to hoard whatever we have, to grab more than we need, to withhold and stop giving to others and frankly to be greedy, and it is this that creates the very shortage we feared. Saving 'for a rainy day' does not promote an attitude of abundance.

To enable abundance to flow in our lives we need clarity. Firstly, we need to be clear about what it is we want. The universe is only too keen to give us our hearts desire, but it cannot do so if we are vague about just what we want. Secondly, we must keep our personal space clear — that is, our physical space as well as our mental space. We should not hoard things we no longer require just because we may need them 'one day' nor should we 'hoard' worries about the future. Clearing out these spaces creates room for something new.

---

### Example

At the time of writing, the UK was facing the threat of protests against high, and rising, oil prices. Several days before the blockades were due to be in place there were queues of cars at almost every petrol station as people panicked that there would not be enough fuel when they really needed to fill their tanks. The result was that many petrol stations ran out of fuel, causing the very problem that people had feared.

Once the protest started to take hold and fuel supplies began to dry up, food supplies started to be threatened. As a result people turned their attention to panic-buying food and other supplies to hoard in case there were shortages. In one extreme instance a man was filmed at the supermarket checkout with twenty-six loaves of bread. The result? Empty supermarket shelves. In the event the protest was over within a few days. The panic-buying had been quite unnecessary except, perhaps, to prove that the fear of shortage was the best way of creating a shortage.

### Exercise

Look around your home for anything you no longer use or need — any clothes, shoes, books, ornaments, CDs or tapes, tins of food, papers; things you haven't used or looked at for years, things that might come in handy 'one day', things you've said you'll get round to sorting out 'one day'. Since this is something that could take some while you might wish to take a room at a time and spend a couple of hours each night or several hours a week to complete your entire home.

Take anything that might be useful to others to a charity shop, anything that could be recycled to the recycling centre and throw away any rubbish.

Consider giving some money — or, if shortage of time is your scarcity conversation, some time — to a charity of your choice. Perhaps you may feel like making a regular commitment, a few pounds or hours a month.

If you want to, share your experience — rather than necessarily the detail of your act of giving — with your companion or buddy on this journey.

❖

*sure you'd dumped me for what's-her-name because she was younger and prettier than me. I felt so empty, cos we did so much together. I missed making love; I missed going out to the pub and all the other things we did. I wanted to hurt you. I blamed you for walking out on me.*

*I haven't been out with another man in all this time — what is it now, 16 years! Now I can see it was me that was losing out all this time. Me I was really hurting. I don't suppose you even knew how I was feeling. How could you know? I realise that relationships don't always last forever, that whatever reason you had for going after what's-her-name was not because there was something wrong with me.*

*Well it's time I got on with my life and let go of this hurt and bitterness. There really is nothing to forgive I know, but I forgive you for the pain I imagined you had caused me and realise I was only causing the pain to myself. And I release us both now to get on with the rest of our lives.*
  *Yours truly*
  *June*

After she had finished writing, she reread the letter, looked at it and then changed 'Yours truly' to 'With love' and then took a match to the letter and allowed it to turn to ashes in the wastepaper bin. She sat back and felt a wave of peace and calm come over her.

### Exercise

Make yourself comfortable. Put on some music and light a candle if that takes your fancy. Take a few deep breaths. Each time you breathe in hold your breath for a few seconds and as you breathe out release your tensions and any thoughts; feel your body and mind relax deeper and deeper.

Think of some past experience in your life; it may be yesterday, something from your childhood, or anywhere in between. An experience where you felt particularly let down, either by yourself or by someone else. Allow yourself to really experience that situation again; allow the emotions and recollections to come back to you. If you feel like crying, great! Allow yourself to cry — just make sure you have a box of tissues to hand.

Become aware of what you are feeling without judging it, or the other person, or yourself. Be aware of the hurt, the anger, the bitterness, the numbness, whatever comes up for you.

When you are ready start to write a letter to that person — remember it could be to yourself. In the letter tell this person precisely how you felt, what you thought. Don't hold anything back. Be as frank and open as you can be. You have nothing to fear from being completely honest. Let everything out. Be sure to do so without blaming them, and without blaming yourself. Just state the facts as you see — or saw — them. You don't have to write good prose or even be grammatically correct. Don't stop to think, just write. And write. And write.

When you have finished putting down on paper all you can, finish off by letting the person know that you forgive them for the wrongs you perceived them to be responsible for. Perhaps you may wish to ask them for their forgiveness. Then stop and feel that forgiveness. Feel it deep within your being.

Then, in a safe manner, burn the letter. Let it all turn to ashes. As the ashes blow or get washed away feel the relief and the release.

If the person is still alive, you may wish to send them a card, or a bunch of flowers, or phone them, or whatever. Then again, you may wish to leave things as they stand. It's your choice.

This exercise can be worth repeating at intervals. For many of us there are probably many events and people in our past that you could do with releasing, many of which you may not be aware of in your day-to-day life. Even if you are not aware of the particular circumstances, even if this was not apparently a major event, this exercise may be practised at any time and is a useful tool to be used from time to time. Even if you have released a particular situation or person, there may be further levels of letting go that you need to visit, just like peeling an onion, so don't assume that because you've written one letter to a particular person, there aren't more inside you waiting to come out!

❖

# Trust and Fear

Trust is inextricably linked to love. In the same way that we cannot fully love someone else unless we truly love ourselves, neither can we really trust others or the universe — God — until we have learned to trust ourselves.

Our life experiences and the negative 'programming' we receive as children often lead us to believe we can trust no one, including ourselves. We learn that if we speak out we may get contradicted or shouted down; that if we give our love to someone we end up getting our heart broken; that perhaps we are sometimes — maybe even, often — 'wrong'. As a result we build barriers to protect ourselves. This leads us to withhold ourselves from others. If we don't speak out — or speak up — we will keep our precious dignity; if we don't get too close to others we will not get hurt.

The greatest men and women in history have been those who don't take life's 'little knocks' as an excuse to give up! Those who have had the greatest impact — both in a positive and a negative way — on humankind are those who understand that a set-back is just a hiccup, a test of their staying power, an invitation to pick themselves up and try again.

It is our fears that keep us from trying again, or from trying something we've never even attempted before. Fear of failure; fear of rejection; fear of feeling foolish; fear of the unknown; fear off not having enough — enough love, money, time or whatever. And sometimes even fear of success!

What is this fear that we allow to run so much of our lives?

Notice that phrase above says 'fear of feeling foolish' not 'fear of being made to look foolish'. That should give us a clue. It is not how other people *make* us feel — no one can make us feel anything — it is how we *choose* to feel. As a result of our interpretation of what happens or what is said, we decide what our response will be, how we feel about it and how we react.

Fear is simply an illusion. It's not real. It is just in our minds; something we have made up — imagined — about what might possibly go wrong. And we are all capable of changing our minds!

When we live our lives in fear of what might 'go wrong' two things happen. Firstly, because we are focussing on it, we are more likely to create those things we fear most. Secondly, we close ourselves off from the love and generosity of God and all but a narrow range of options from the infinite possibilities that the universe has at its disposal. We simply put ourselves in a frame of mind that only sees what we expect to see.

As spiritual beings on the road of enlightenment, there should be no room for fear. Protecting ourselves from perceived threats is itself a barrier to enlightenment, because in protecting ourselves in this way we are cutting off a whole range of other options and opportunities, and we are putting up a barrier between ourselves and the light. We are called on to live our lives with an open heart, aware that the universe provides us with everything we need just when we need it, that nothing is out of place or out of time. Our 'higher self' beseeches us to trust the universe, to trust ourselves and to trust others.

It can be a difficult lesson to learn especially when things are not going the way we want them to go. However, it is at times when the going gets tough that we have most to learn, if we are willing to do so — if we are open. It may help if we understand that there is a reason for everything, even if we do not know the reason at the time.

Then again, what seems like a disaster at the time might in hindsight be viewed as a blessing in disguise. The argument with a partner that leads to you forming a stronger relationship; missing the train only to find your appointment has been cancelled anyway; the failed interview for the job you had set your heart on only to land a better job a few weeks later.

If we can learn to trust the universe and trust that whatever occurs in our lives is there for a reason, we will begin to find that life is a lot less stressful and we have no need of worry or fear about the future. Even if we don't understand what the reason is at the time, we know that there is a reason for everything and we trust that we will become aware of that reason in good time.

As we learn to trust and go with the flow of life, we begin to find that our lives run more smoothly, that we are calmer and more at peace with life whatever it brings, that our relationships are easier, that there is a certain synchronicity in much of what occurs to us. We find there is no longer any need to 'play games' with ourselves, or with others. We can be more open and honest. As we begin to trust ourselves we discover — or maybe rediscover — our creative abilities and our intuition. We find that there is no longer any need to try and force life to do what we want the way we want it.

---

### Example

Joe was self-employed. He had never been able to plan his workload as his work seemed to come in when he least expected it. There were times when he started feeling a little desperate that he had no work. He had rung all his contacts, had chased all those who had expressed an interest in his services but still the work was not coming in. He still had a mortgage and bills to pay. In his mind — at an intellectual level — Joe understood the need to trust that the universe would provide all that he needed. At an intellectual level he believed this; but it didn't stop him from fretting.

He remembered the old adage that 'God helps those who help themselves', and, from one of the personal development courses he attended, the phrase 'the universe applauds action not thought' came to mind. Joe also knew that if he asked the universe for help but then hung onto his 'problem' by constantly worrying as to how and when it would be 'fixed' he was not allowing the universe to support him. However, it was easier said than done for him to let go of the issue.

It was clear to him that his present course of action was not working, but he felt sure he should be doing something and not simply waiting for the universe to deliver him a job on a plate. Perhaps, Joe figured, if I start to look for a full-time job, it will demonstrate my commitment to getting some work. And so the following Sunday he bought two of the Sunday papers that were best known for their job advertisements. He scoured the ads marking those that he best seemed suited for. He was not impressed as many of the jobs would mean moving home and, having been his own boss for eight years he didn't relish working for someone else. However, he knew it had to be done and he set to with a light heart. Having reread the ads several times he found six jobs that vaguely interested him and so he printed off six copies of his CV and wrote an accompanying letter for each one and posted them off.

A week later, Joe was wondering what had happened with his job applications when the phone rang. It was one of his former work colleagues offering him a six-month contract. No interview. It was his for the asking. He never heard from any of the jobs he had applied for.

### Exercise

Take yourself off to a place where you can get some peace and quiet. Play some quiet classical music if you wish. Sit down and make yourself comfortable. Take a few deep breaths; breathe in as far as you can, hold your breath for a few seconds and then let it go gently. Repeat this three or four times and allow your body to relax more each time. Quieten your mind and allow all thoughts to float away.

Now take your notebook and a pen and recall one or two examples of when you've been striving for something, trying really hard, and the universe has not been coming up with the goods. Maybe all your efforts seemed to be producing the opposite of what you wanted. Perhaps you kept trying the same thing with the same result. Now think forward to when you finally achieved what you actually wanted. What changed? Was it simply patience? Did you try a different tack? Maybe you gave up. Perhaps you changed your mind about what you wanted. Write down all you can recall about the situation, about what changed, what worked and what didn't work, and what you can learn from the situation.

You might like to repeat this exercise for other situations as well, perhaps at some later time.

Once again, if you are working with a buddy you may wish to compare notes.

❖

# Balance and Disease

The universe is at all times in a state of balance. When something happens to alter that state of equilibrium then the universe takes corrective action to restore the balance. Our own lives, too, are seeking to find a state of balance, although it is only by experiencing extremes that we are able to fully appreciate balance.

When we veer to one extreme in our lives the universe moves to make whatever adjustments are necessary to help us regain the state of balance. If we resist the changes then we tend to become discontented, stressed or ill.

Our lives often swing from one extreme to another like a pendulum. This is often necessary for two reasons. Firstly it can enable us to find a 'happy medium', somewhere between the two extremes where we find contentment. Secondly, we need to experience one extreme in order to fully appreciate the other. Without scarcity we would not be able to fully understand abundance, without loneliness we would not know companionship; similarly with fear and love, despair and hope, suspicion and trust, sadness and joy, illness and good health, hot and cold, left and right, light and dark.

We experience disease — or dis-ease — when we are out of balance in some area of our lives; when we are not in a state of well-being or wholeness. It is not caused by factors outside ourselves but by our own state of being. Of course, outside factors do have some bearing on our health. Germs and toxins are around us all the time. But it is our own state of well-being or otherwise that determines whether or not we are susceptible to any particular disease at any particular time.

It is generally well accepted that we are more likely to succumb to an illness when we are rundown or stressed. For instance, a cold or flu is often our body's way of telling us to slow down or take a rest; cancer is sometimes associated with sustained, unresolved stress or suppressed anger; obesity and bulimia can often be due to an acute lack of self-esteem.

Other diseases, too, can be symptomatic of suppressed emotions or feelings. Poor eyesight can be an indication of something we are not prepared to 'look at' either within our own life or our surroundings. Problems with our ears may suggest there is something we do not wish to hear. Diseases of the genitalia may indicate we have issues about sex generally, or procreation, or our own sexuality.

More and more people are recognising the efficacy of holistic — whole person — healing rather than treating just the symptoms. Remedies and therapies such as Reiki, Bach flower remedies, hypnotherapy, homoeopathy and Shiatsu all recognise the importance of treating the whole person, and many recognise the importance of mental attitude both in the cause as well as the treatment of diseases — what used to be thought of as psychosomatic illnesses.

Our bodies and our subconscious always know better than our conscious minds what is in our best interests. When we experience discomfort it is our body's way of telling us we are doing something that is not in our best interests. If we ignore the discomfort it will increase, and if we continue to ignore it then the discomfort will eventually become a disease.

### Example

Joyce was one of those people who is always on the go. Not only did she work hard but she had a busy social diary, too. On one occasion when she began to feel a little under the weather, she told herself she could not afford the time to be ill. She had a particularly busy schedule for the next ten days before she went to America for a week's trip. She continued seeing her clients and with her social events, getting more tired by the day, but she was determined she would not be

## Forgiveness

Often misunderstood, forgiveness is not about allowing someone to 'get away with it' — whatever 'it' may be, and whatever may be meant by 'getting away'. Forgiveness really means releasing and letting go of a situation or a person, and not allowing it or them to have a hold over us any longer. When we hold on to something or someone that is passed we create a blockage or resentment, and this can sometimes build up in our bodies as excess fat, or stress, cancer, or some other illness. At best it keeps us in the past and stops us moving forward in our lives.

If we continue to feel resentment towards someone or a situation we believe has somehow 'wronged' us long after it has passed, we are often prevented from seeing the greater opportunities that life is offering us. The person we are hurting most is ourselves, whilst the other person is often unaware of our feelings and is getting on with their life regardless.

The first step to forgiving — or releasing, letting go, healing — is to accept the situation as it is; accept that nothing you can do is going to change it. It's happened. It's gone. It's in the past.

Then become aware of your feelings — of loss, of hurt, of being let down, injustice, guilt, whatever. Just let them be. Allow yourself to really feel them. Take your time. If you feel like crying, then cry; crying can be very therapeutic, and tears can have a wonderful cleansing effect.

One effective way to release events from the past is to write a letter to the person at the root of the situation. It may be someone who you feel injured or hurt you in some way, it may be someone you let down, or it might be a time you let yourself down. The letter is seldom, if ever, sent to the person concerned, so you are free to write whatever comes into your heart — not with a sense of blame and rancour, but in a responsible and honest manner. The letter may be burned — safely! — or written on toilet paper and flushed away.

Even if we don't harbour a grudge or resentment for some past event or person, most of us are still 'carrying' something about a number of situations and people from our past, including ourselves; things that we are perhaps not even aware of in our daily lives. Even though they may have little effect on our lives on a day-to-day basis we may still find it helps us to release these things. We may need to revisit some things more than once to fully release ourselves from its power, each time releasing just a little more of the situation.

---

### Example

June was naturally very hurt when her first real boyfriend, Tom, went off with another girl. She was a rather private person and she felt that, at twenty-five, she had been a 'late starter'. For years after the split, in almost every conversation with those friends that knew them both she would somehow find a way to mention Tom. It was obvious she had never forgiven him or forgotten what she perceived 'he had done to her'. After fifteen years she was still bitter and in all that time she had never had another relationship. Tom was completely unaware of her feelings and had been getting on with his life. The only person that June was hurting was herself.

Her friends had no idea how to tell June that they felt this harping on about Tom was unhealthy and in all those years she had never had another boyfriend. Eventually after advice from her local minister, June decided to write to Tom.

> *Dear Tom*
> 
> *I don't really know where to begin. It really hurt when you left me. I was left wondering what I'd done wrong. I really hated you. After all we'd meant to each other. I was*

## Enlightenment for Beginners ■ 75

beaten by a mere cold. And she won! At least, she didn't succumb to the flu, or whatever it was, before she got to America. However, once she arrived with her friends in the United States and she began to relax, the flu hit her with a vengeance and she spent the whole of the week in bed under the ministration of her friends.

### Exercise

Find yourself a place to get quiet and relaxed. Play some calming music and light a candle or two if you wish. Sit still and close your eyes. Take a deep breath; hold your breath for a few seconds and then breathe out, feeling all tension leave your body and allowing all thoughts to float away. Repeat this a few times allowing yourself to become more and more relaxed each time.

Take your notebook and think of a time when something in your life was out of balance. It may have been when everything seemed to be going 'wrong' for you, or it might just be that one or two things did not seem to be going as planned. Consider for the present some past event rather than something that is going on for you right now. Relive the events. Write down what was happening for you, how you felt, what you did. How long did the situation go on for? Were there some early warnings? Did the situation get worse? How was it finally resolved? Think about what you might have done differently when you received the early warning, and how the outcome may have been different. Be careful not to 'beat yourself up' about the situation — this is an opportunity to learn from the past not to give yourself a hard time and say 'if only…'. It is important to our spiritual awakening to learn to view life's little set-backs as opportunities to learn and grow, not as occasions for recriminations or self-pity.

You may wish to share and discuss what you have discovered with your buddy or special friend.

You may also find it helpful to revisit this exercise at some later date and take a look at situations that you are dealing with at the time.

# Free Will

Even though the lessons we want to learn and the experiences we wish to have are decided before we reincarnate, this does not mean that our lives are predestined. We all have the free will to act or not act at every moment of every day as we so choose. This may mean that some of the plans we made before coming back to Earth are temporarily put into disarray, either as a result of our own or someone else's choices.

However, our plans are seldom completely destroyed. We will inevitably create a 'plan B' and find another soul to work with or another situation that will support us in attaining our goal or learning the lesson.

As we move further along the path of enlightenment and become more consciously aware of the help we are receiving from our unseen friends, we realise that the situations that are presented to us are simply lessons placed there to help us in our life's journey, not obstacles to be overcome. Once we learn to align our will with the divine will and learn to trust the perfection of the universe and the perfection of our own lives, we begin to find it more easy to accept each event that occurs in our lives as an opportunity to learn and grow rather than an experience to be suffered. We always have the free will to say 'no' to a situation that is presented to us. We can find ways to ignore, evade or bypass the situation until it goes away. However, sooner or later another situation will arise that will invite us again to learn whatever lessons it was there to support us in. Each time we decline such an invitation the next is less subtle and more confrontational, making it harder to ignore. This will be repeated as many times as is needed until we finally learn that lesson.

### Example

Joanna had been 'on the spiritual path' for a few years. She had been in a long-term relationship that had been getting stale. She knew that she had to end it for the good of them both, and in particular for her own spiritual development. Probably the most difficult thing she had ever done in her life, she ended the relationship, and after three years alone she knew she was ready for a new relationship. This time she felt sure it would be with someone who was also 'on the path'.

She met a wonderful man, Peter, with whom she instantly 'clicked' and with whom she could discuss almost anything. They very quickly fell in love and phoned each other at least twice a day and exchanged at least as many email messages. So many things seemed to suggest to them both that they were meant for each other. It was like nothing she had ever experienced before.

Then Joanna found an old pattern of behaviour reappearing; she found herself worrying that Peter might 'go off' her. She would 'chew over' little things he'd said on the phone or in his emails and she started seeking his assurance. Peter, who had his own insecurities, found Joanna's neediness rather threatening. Eventually, he broke off their next date in an email. Joanna was stunned. He had suggested it was not final but more of a 'cooling off' period, but whenever Joanna phoned he was friendly but aloof, and not ready to see her again. She was confused. Assuming he needed his own space for a while, but confident they would get back together before too long, Joanna was determined to be patient.

As she described it afterwards, she felt like she went to Hell and back. There were times when she felt there was no point in carrying on; sometimes she wanted to phone Peter and tell him where to stick himself! Through it all she realised there was a reason for all that was going on, even if she couldn't see it at the time.

Finally, after three months, Joanna rang Peter, who

seemed surprised to hear from her. They talked about meeting but he was rather non-committal; he said he'd write to her. Puzzled, she waited for the letter. Later, she could recall little of what the letter said, except the phrase 'sorry it didn't work out'. Well, now at least she knew; what he had been unable to say to her face or on the phone, Peter eventually said in a letter.

Much to her surprise, Joanna quickly got over her grief. Her friends, who she felt she had bored to tears with her tales of woe over the previous few months, were a great support to her. She realised that a man who could not tell her the truth to her face was not someone she wanted to be with anyway.

Slowly, it became obvious to her that her months of loneliness and pain and anguish had helped her to work through her neediness and the fear of losing someone; that the time had been necessary for her healing. She began to see the perfection in all that had happened in that short relationship. She realised that she had unconsciously invited someone into her life to help her through this 'hang-up' and that Peter had answered her call; that all those little signs had been there to 'trigger' her emotions and responses; that Peter had acted in just the ways that were necessary to support her in finally getting it out of her system; that even though relationships were 'meant to be' they might only be for just a short while. Yes, she could truly see perfection in what had happened.

Just a couple of months later Joanna was to meet another man with whom she gradually fell in love. She found the experience with Peter made her far more aware of the insecurities of her new love as well as her own, and she was able to give him the space he needed within the relationship without clinging; indeed she found having space within the relationship was helpful to her too.

### Exercise

Find yourself a comfortable place to do the following exercise. Relax. Breathe deeply. Play some relaxing music if that helps you. Light a candle and an incense stick, too, if that is what you like. Relax. Relax.

Think of one of the people who has been in your life or some situation with whom or with which you had a lot of difficulty. It needn't be a personal relationship; it could be, for example, a neighbour, someone you work with, or an authority figure. For the present it would be better to look at a relationship that is over rather than someone with whom you are still having difficulties. Write down what you find most difficult about the person, how and when it started, what you have done to calm things, what you have done to irritate the situation. Now take a look at that relationship from the position of responsibility. Ask yourself, 'What lessons or experiences did this person come to help me with?' 'Why did I invite them into my life?' 'What is there for me to learn here?' Write down what comes to you in your notebook.

When you have finished the exercise, you may find it helpful to compare notes with your special friend or buddy if you are working with someone else.

You may wish to repeat this exercise with other people and situations at any time if it helps. With practice what can be most helpful is to look at situations and relationships that are current for you. Learn to accept the situation just as it is without judging it or yourself or others involved as 'wrong' or 'bad'. Ask yourself the same questions.

❖

# Mirror Principle

The mirror principle teaches us that we only ever see in others what there is within ourselves. Many of us may recall the childhood taunt, 'It takes one to know one'. If we see other people in our lives as kind, generous and loving then that is a reflection of our own ways of being. On the other hand, if people seem distant or unfriendly, negative or unreasonable, angry or aggressive, then that is how we appear to them. The simple truth is that we only recognise a trait or quality in someone else if it is one we have ourselves. If it is not something we have within ourselves then either we simply don't notice it or we don't react to it.

This can be a difficult principle to accept, particularly if the trait we recognise in someone else is one we consider to be a negative one. 'I'm not like that at all!' we cry when faced with someone who presses all our buttons. However, if we look deep enough, we will be able to find some similarity, some reason why this trait so annoys us. It may well be something we have suppressed since childhood.

The people — and indeed the pets — in our lives are there to help us see ourselves the way we really are, the way other people see us, rather than the way we would like to be seen or the way we think other people see us. They are there to help us work through whatever issues we have with those ways of being, to accept them as part of us and change them if we feel that is required. Very often we will find that if we change our attitude to the other person, not only will we feel less ill at ease about the situation but the other person will also automatically change their way of being.

Similarly, the state of our homes and possessions and the

way we dress are mirrors of what is going on inside us. As well as being indicators of our general level of self-esteem, the state of particular items can indicate specific blockages or problems. Broken clocks or watches suggest we have some issue with time. Dripping pipes or radiators can be a symptom of unshed tears or problems with our 'waterworks'. Hoarding anything is a good indication of a blockage of some sort. Getting rid of unused items is an excellent way to create room for something new in our life. And anything broken needs to be mended or discarded.

### Example

After the breakup of her marriage June lived alone with her West Highland Terrier dog, Terry. She couldn't understand why Terry was so nervous and clinging. Given the chance, Terry would follow June around the house, and whenever she had visitors he would be especially jealous and demand her attention. He would try to keep June in his sight all the time, as though her friends were likely to take June away from him.

'This is not like me,' claimed June. For three years she denied any similarity between the behaviour of her dog and herself, but it kept nagging away at her. As she worked on trying to find answers she began to see some hazy picture emerging. Yes, she had been very shy as a child and as a young adult, often too shy to go out on dates. When she did pluck up the courage to say 'yes' when asked out on a date she would immediately assume that this was the right boy for her, and would smother the relationship before it had a chance to get started. But she was over all that now. Maybe Terry had been more affected by the breakup of her marriage than she had realised.

Finally, she accepted that, whatever it was, there was still something unresolved and that Terry was a reflection of some part of her subconscious. There was something there that he had to teach her even if she didn't know what is was. She asked the universe for help in ascertaining what it was and in resolving it and trusted that in the fullness of time this would become clear to her and would get resolved.

## Exercise

Take yourself off to your favourite place for quiet and contemplation. Light a candle and some incense and put on some soft music if you wish to. Close your eyes. Take a deep breath and hold it for a few seconds, then breathe out slowly. Repeat several more times. Visualise your body and mind relaxing with each breath.

Now take your notebook and consider some of the people, and perhaps the pets, in your life whose actions or ways of being you find difficult to handle. Also take a look at those people you particularly admire in your life. Consider each person or animal one at a time. What are they trying to tell you about yourself, your relationships with others and your relationship with yourself? Are they perhaps picking up on signals you are unconsciously sending out? Note down any thoughts that come to you, however vague they may be. Mark those that make you feel most uncomfortable. Consider how you might be contributing to the situation. Write down your further thoughts and feelings.

If you wish to, share what you have learned with your buddy or special friend.

You may wish to work with just one person or pet to begin with and come back to others some time later.

❖

# Thoughts Create

Understand that our thoughts create our reality. This is the one of the keys of spiritual awakening. Negative and limiting beliefs keep us from achieving all that we are capable of, from manifesting our true destiny, from performing the role we came into this world to fulfil. Worse still, toxic thoughts can create confusion within our own lives and with others, misunderstandings, bitterness, resentment, fighting and bullying, which eventually lead to wars.

Everything is a choice. We can choose to have positive, life-affirming thoughts, or we can choose negative, toxic thoughts. Much has been built up around the power of positive thinking, and it is often treated as though it is an end in itself and a panacea for all ills. There are quite simply many things that cannot be achieved by 'positive thinking' alone. The positive thinking ideology tends to deny reality. What is important is not the doctrine of positive thinking, but focussing on what is positive — it may sound like a subtle distinction but it's an important one. For example, positive thinking is unlikely to turn a rainy day into a sunny one, but focussing on the positive can make that rainy day outing just as enjoyable as if the day had been a sunny one. How often have we heard someone complain on a rainy day, 'Oh, isn't this weather miserable!' Well, no, the weather isn't miserable. The weather has no feelings at all, neither miserable nor happy. What the person is really saying is, 'I feel miserable because it is raining.' That's their choice.

It is one of the principles of the universe that whatever we focus our thoughts on expands. If we focus on what isn't working in our life or worrying about things we don't want to happen, guess what? We get more of what we don't want! How much better, then, to focus on what we do want, what is going right, on being loving and compassionate and helpful, on how we may best serve others!

Worry and guilt are two of the most futile and self-indulgent exercises we human beings undertake. Worrying about the past — 'Did I say (or do) the right thing?' 'Should I have...?' 'What if I had...?' etc. — is so utterly pointless because there is no way it is going to change the past. Whatever happened, happened. It is gone, past, done and dusted. Worrying about what might happen in the future is equally absurd as it has never been known to change things for the better. What our worrying is most likely to achieve is a state of mind that, firstly, is more likely to bring about the very thing we fear and, secondly, creates in ourselves stress and disease. Worry and guilt are simply a waste of energy.

The idea that our thoughts can create something material is often met with incredulity at first. However, it may not seem so unlikely if we realise that everything that has ever been created starts with a thought. A new product starts off as an idea by its inventor or designer; a new baby begins as a thought by its parents. Wars, record-breaking achievements, inventions, mass murders, artistic creations and all human accomplishments — whether positive or negative — all begin with a thought by someone, somewhere.

Most people will have noticed at one time or another how our feelings and emotions can be transmitted to others. Whether they're what we consider to be 'positive' emotions such as love, happiness, enthusiasm, compassion, or so-called 'negative' emotions such as anger, guilt, jealousy, depression and so on, others can — and often do — pick up on our emotions and then similarly pass them on to others. Not only are our feelings and emotions transmitted to others, they are often amplified on the way.

Given the possible effect of thoughts, we need to protect ourselves from the negative thoughts and feelings of others. A simple and effective way of doing this is given in the chapter 'Prayer and Meditation'.

---

### Example

George and Linda wanted to try out the 'good life' and after much planning and thinking bought a small farm with a few acres of land where they raised a few animals. Linda was a city-girl with no experience of farming; George had been brought up on a farm and knew a lot about the things that could go wrong on a farm.

Every year for the first five years they attempted to make some hay from their small acreage. Each year George imagined all the things that could go wrong. He worried and fretted that the contractor wouldn't turn up at the right time to cut the grass; that he wouldn't come back in time to turn and bale the hay; that the weather would turn before they had got the hay in and it would be ruined; he imagined all manner of ills befalling them. Sure enough, every year their crop of hay was less than perfect. Linda couldn't stand all this worrying. She found the negative atmosphere oppressive and found it difficult to maintain her own optimism in the face of such an onslaught.

Whilst she didn't understand why it should work that way, Linda was convinced it was no coincidence that they always got a poor crop of hay, especially as none of their neighbours suffered the same fate. There had to be a link between the results they achieved and George's negative thinking. But how? George imagining it raining could hardly cause it to rain could it? It was several years before she found a possible explanation.

Linda had come to accept that on a spiritual level we could, and indeed do, communicate with each other, and that we had a 'higher self' that already knew the answers we were searching for. On this basis, it occurred to Linda, it was quite possible – and even likely – that in his negative state George was not open to the counsel of his higher self urging him when to call the contractor, and that the contractor subconsciously picked up on George's desire to 'fail' and acted accordingly. It may not be the complete answer, argued Linda, but it could explain things.

### Exercise

Find a quiet place. Put on some classical or 'new age' music if you require. Make yourself comfortable. Take a few deep breaths. Breathe in deeply and hold your breath for a few seconds; breath out slowly. Repeat this a few times. Relax both your body and your mind.

Think of an example of where negative thinking on your part or that of someone else produced just the results that were feared. Perhaps when a relationship 'failed' in a similar way to previous ones, or when you 'failed' a job interview because you didn't expect to get the job, or when a small disagreement escalated into a full-scale row 'because they always do'. Then in your notebook write down the circumstance of the situation. Perhaps you weren't consciously aware of the negative influences on the situation. Consider how those thoughts may have actually created the results. How might a different mental attitude have produced different results? Write down any reaction you have to this or any insights you have gained.

If you wish to, share your insights with your buddy or companion if you have one.

❖

# Words and Affirmations

Just as our thoughts create our reality, so too they determine the words we use; positive thoughts inevitably result in us using words that empower and encourage, negative thoughts in words that restrain and discourage. However, it can work the other way round, too. By changing the words we use, we can affect our whole attitude to the events in our lives.

Words to avoid include negative and unempowering words such as can't, which invariably really means *won't*, never, problem, failure, unfair, which as well as being better expressed in a more positive or a neutral manner also indicate to us that there is an element of judgement in our thinking and attitude; 'guilt' words such as could, should and would, which keep us focussed on regrets of what we did or did not do in the past and are better replaced by *will* and a resolve not to repeat past actions with which we would prefer not to be associated; judgemental words like good and bad, right and wrong, pathetic, which show our lack of acceptance of life just as it is.

We can turn around our negative thinking by the use of affirmations. Affirmations can be a simple and effective method for creating in our lives the things we desire. An affirmation is a statement about something positive that already exists. It is in the first person; it is in the present tense and it is positive.

If we turn our desires into affirmations and repeat them out loud regularly we can 're-program' our subconscious so that it sees only the positive images we are projecting and creates a new reality based on positive thoughts instead of the negative ones that many of us have used for so much of our lives. Affirmations need to be repeated for at least twenty-one days preferably twice each day in order to re-program the subconscious mind. And the wording of the affirmations is important, too. Vague phrases will at best produce vague results; powerful phrases will produce powerful results.

Powerful affirmations begin with words such as: 'I deserve…', 'I am…', 'I have…'. For example, 'I deserve the best that life has to offer', 'I am a successful and prolific writer', 'I have a happy and loving relationship'. Your ego, your inner Doubting Thomas will feel most uncomfortable with these at first. However, it is important to ignore these doubts and continue with your affirmations. Recognise the doubts for what they are and continue regardless.

You should not start your affirmations with vague phrases such as: 'I want…' or 'I believe…' or 'I will…'. These are all based on the future not the present and all they will achieve is to increase your want or your belief rather than bring about the positive change you are seeking.

If your circumstances or desires change then you can always amend your affirmations — provided you don't do so too often!

---

## Example

Without giving away his life story, Jerry was a healer and had a rather small income. He had undertaken one or two personal development courses and although he was fairly self-aware he didn't feel he was really 'firing on all cylinders' and achieving all that he might. He was mindful that his smoking was a drain on his limited income, that it certainly did not improve his health and that it was, perhaps, incongruous with his vocation. And, although he was popular and had a number of good friends and acquaintances in the gay community, he wanted someone special in his life, something that always seemed to elude him.

After considering the things that were really important in his life, writing them down, crossing some out, writing new things, rewording some of them, he wrote down the following list of affirmations:

> *I know I am already whole and I need chase after nothing in order to be complete.*
> *I am open and receptive to the good and abundance of the universe.*
> *I no longer crave cigarettes; I have no need for nicotine.*
> *I release all negative and limiting thoughts and beliefs.*
> *I have an open, honest, intimate and loving relationship with a man who has similar values and interests to mine.*

Aware, too, that some greater self-love and self-esteem would not go amiss, particularly in his healing, he added:

> *I love myself because I am a child of God.*

Then, he rewrote the list neatly on a new sheet of paper which he kept by his bedside, and he recited his affirmations first thing each morning and last thing each night before retiring to bed.

### Exercise

Find yourself a quiet and relaxing space. Play some soft music if you like. Light a candle, perhaps. Take a few deep, really deep breaths. Each time you breathe out feel you body relax deeper and deeper. Allow your mind to relax, too.

Think of the things you are aiming for in life. Not just the material things, like a new home or car, but your spiritual aims as well. Write down the things you most desire in your notebook. Then consider carefully which are the most important ones for you and turn these into affirmations — i.e. statements of fact that are in the first person, in the present tense and positive.

You may wish to discuss your affirmations with your special friend. This can be especially helpful to find the most effective and most powerful wording. Then again, if you wish to keep them to yourself, that's fine too.

When you are happy with them rewrite your affirmations on a separate sheet of paper and keep it beside your bed. Read or recite your affirmations out loud first thing every morning and last thing at night before you go to sleep. You will find they become more powerful if you commit them to memory rather than read them from the piece of paper. And reciting them out loud can help the re-programming because you are bringing another of your senses into play – your hearing. You may also find reciting them to yourself in the mirror makes them even more powerful. You will probably find it difficult to say positive things about yourself to begin with, but don't allow that to stop you. Those negative doubts will start to disappear as you persevere.

❖

# Consequences

No, this is not about the party game where you write the first line of a story on a piece of paper, fold it over and then pass it on for the next person to write the next line, and so on until the last person writes the consequence and you end up with a nonsense story!

As mentioned before, everything we do, every word we speak and every thought we have has some result on our wider world — a consequence. Or, to put it another more familiar way, what goes round comes around.

The idea of consequences can, perhaps, best be illustrated by the law of gravity; the consequence of throwing something into the air is that it comes back down to earth due to the force of gravity. There is no 'right' or 'wrong' about it, there is no judgement, it is not about punishment, it just is. So, too, with the consequences of our actions and our thoughts. They are without judgement, simply a case of cause and effect. Whatever we sow, we shall reap. What goes around comes around. The same thing, however you care to think about it.

A consequence, or effect, may occur a split second after the related cause, or it may be days, weeks or years after, or even in some future lifetime.

This is what some people refer to as karma. However, as there are often misunderstandings and differences of opinion as to what is meant by karma, and connotations of 'good' or 'bad', the term 'consequence' or 'cause and effect' may be easier to understand. Karma should not be considered as a punishment or reward but simply as a lesson.

Until we recognise the effect that our actions, our words and our thoughts have on the wider world, until we accept responsibility for everything that happens in our lives and act accordingly, we may as well be walking around asleep.

Unless we understand how we interact with our surroundings and with other people, and how our thoughts and energies are transmitted to others, we communicate our energies to those around us without realising the effect it may be having on them and on the world as a whole. Whilst we continue to blame others for the circumstances in which we finds ourselves and for what happens in our lives, so long as we complain that life is unfair, or that we don't have enough, we are in danger of spreading negative energies without being aware of the — possibly dire — consequence it may be having on others and the wider world.

As mentioned earlier, our emotions and feelings are not only transmitted to others, but they frequently become amplified as they move on. Our anger and frustration when expressed in 'negative' ways such as shouting, trading insults and blaring car horns, may lead to brawls, road rage and eventually to mass murders and wars. Our greed and expressions that we do not have enough can lead to burglary and world shortages. Envy and jealousy of others' achievements and accomplishments may result in vandalism.

However, once we wake up to our responsibilities and become conscious, we become more aware of the effect our thoughts, words and actions may be having outside ourselves. That is not to say we don't become angry, or depressed, or wish for more — although such feelings do tend to reduce when we are on the path of enlightenment — but we hopefully find ways of expressing any negative thoughts and emotions we may have in ways that limit the negative effect they have on others. And we create more opportunities to express our gratitude, our love and our joy.

It is therefore important for us to be conscious of our feelings and aware of what we are thinking, so that we do not allow our negative energies to be released unconsciously into the wider world.

## Example

Consequences do not just apply to individuals, they also apply to nations, corporations, football clubs, families, indeed to any group of people. There are those who consider that Britain's popularity as a place of refuge for asylum seekers and economic migrants is a natural result of its eighteenth century colonisation of the world — a simple result of the law of cause and effect.

Once again, this is not about the 'rightness' or 'wrongness' of Britain's colonisation of the world, the way in which it treated the indigenous people of those countries it colonised, or of the choice of Britain as a place for asylum or refuge, it is simply a statement of the situation as it is.

## Exercise

At this time in the evolution of humankind and the Earth, it is possible for many of us to transmute our karmic debts without repayment provided, firstly, that we ask; secondly, that the soul to whom the debt is 'owed' is in agreement; and thirdly, that it would be for the highest good of all parties concerned. Of course, if we wish to be released from any karmic debts we owe, we must also agree to release others from any debts they may owe us, again, provided they ask and that it is for the highest good of all concerned. However, since such requests occur at a soul level, we may not be consciously aware of them nor of our response.

In a meditative state — you may wish to refer to the section headed 'Prayer and Meditation – how to meditate' — visualise a silver-blue flame. Focus your attention on the flame and bring into its glow all those to whom you owe a karmic debt of one form or another. If you have trouble visualising people just *imagine* them all there together in the flame. Give yourself plenty of time and when you are ready, using whatever words feel suitable to you, ask them to release you from the debt you owe them. Then thank them for coming, for their time and for considering your request. Give them all your love. Do not dwell on it. Come out of your meditation trusting and knowing that if it be for the highest good then you will be released from those debts.

Such a release will free you to be able to serve others in ever greater ways.

❖

# Unity

If there is one principle, one spiritual tenet, that perhaps best sums up enlightenment or spirituality, it is arguably that of oneness or unity.

Wherever we look our world appears to be one of 'us' and 'them'. And wherever there is an 'us and them' mentality we find misunderstandings and conflict, for example between Christian and Jew, old and young, protestant and catholic, male and female, rich and poor, disabled and able-bodied, white and black, political 'left' and political 'right', workers and management, companies and governments protecting their own interests. It is as though we have been conditioned from an early age to look for differences between ourselves and others rather than for similarities, even where the similarities are far greater and far more numerous than the differences.

This idea of being different — of separateness — is, in fact, just another illusion. In spirit, we are all part of the one divine love that created us all, linked by the one energy that flows through all of us and all of life. Perhaps it may help us to understand the idea of our co-dependency if we realise that the air we breathe has already passed through many people, animals and plants before it gets to our bodies. We are all connected, although the rather heavy energies of the Earth plane make it difficult for us to be aware of this truth all the time.

If we can recognise the truth of this then our lives on Earth can be less stressful and less competitive. We realise that rivalry between individuals and between nations does nothing to create a world of harmony, cooperation and peace.

Only by working in cooperation with each other, both individually and internationally, can we ever hope to bring about a fair and just world, one that works for everyone.

I do not wish to suggest that healthy competition should be avoided; indeed competition can be very beneficial if it helps us strive towards higher goals or achieves something that would not have been achieved without the added impetus. However, we need to be clear about the distinction between healthy competition and conflict.

The principle of oneness reminds us that it is important for us to understand that wars, conflicts, poverty, starvation and natural disasters in any part of the world are of concern to all of us whether or not we are affected directly. Our response to situations such as these is a statement of our commitment to resolving them. Whether our response is to pray or meditate for resolution, or is in terms of financial or moral support is not so important as the fact that we make a positive response.

### Example

One simple but very powerful illustration of the principal of unity is the felling of the rainforests in Brazil. The need or desire for the income derived by deforestation by a single country has an impact on all of humanity. The rainforests are vital to the survival of humankind, and by some estimates the amount of oxygen produced in the world has been reduced by twenty percent in the last fifty years due to the loss of the rainforests.

### Exercise

Find yourself a quiet spot. Put on some quiet music and light a candle. Take a deep breath; breathe in as far as you can; hold your breath for a few moments and then breathe out. Feel your body and your mind relax. Repeat this a few more times allowing your body and mind to relax further each time.

Now take your notebook. You may wish to consider what,

if anything, international competitive sports events might contribute to the oneness of our world. Perhaps there are some sports that make a positive contribution and others that detract from oneness. If so, what are the differences between those sports that help engender oneness and those that don't? What is missing in those sports that create separation rather than harmony?

Look at ways in which you create conflict rather than harmony in your life. Make a list. Consider what differences you could make to create a win-win situation for all concerned. You may want to consider just one or two situations from your list, or you may find a common thread running through them all where making a single change would affect several different situations.

If you wish you may compare notes and share with your buddy or companion anything you have learned in this exercise.

❖

# Ego and Attachment

Our ego is our greatest opponent when it comes to enlightenment, and indeed the path of spirituality is in part about learning to tame our ego. On the one hand our ego wants us to believe that we are special and better and set apart from everyone else. On the other hand it frequently stops us from achieving all that we are capable of by trying to convince us we're not up to it.

If this seems like a contradiction, perhaps this is because that is just what our ego intends! What ego wants most is to be in control of our lives. It thrives on our confusion, fear, jealousy and discord because through these it has control of us. A spiritual life based on love, trust, harmony and calm is not at all to the liking of ego, and it will do whatever it can to persuade us that this is not the true path.

In a contrary sort of way ego believes it has our best interests at heart and that our interest is best served by protecting us from ourselves and from others. Ego wants us to believe that it is the voice of 'reality' when in fact its responses are really based on fear — fear of the unknown and fear of ego's loss of control over us.

Ego is afraid of the unknown. It likes to keep us on a tried and tested path. Ego believes that only by us controlling our environment can we really be secure and happy; hence its need to control us. It tries to convince us that we need more of something, and then when we have more of that something it will tell us we need even more of it, or more of something else. It wants us to be discontented, always seeking something outside ourselves. However, this is all based on the falsehood that we are separate from our environment, that we are in some way deficient.

The art of taming ego is that whenever our ego sticks its head up expressing its doubts and fears masquerading as the voice of reality, we need firstly to recognise that it is ego trying to keep us stuck in the past and then acknowledge it and thank ego kindly for its concern and simply tell it it is not wanted right now. With practice, like most spiritual exercises, this can become second nature to us, and it is a very effective tool.

The truth is that ego is living in the past. Ego had an important part to play in the early evolution of humankind enabling us to handle situations of 'fight or flight' where the choice of reaction could literally be a matter of life and death. In modern life where most of us do not face life-and-death situations on a daily basis ego only inhibits our growth and those who seek a spiritual life need to learn to take action in the here and now rather than react according to what happened in the past.

One of the other characteristics of ego is that it has great difficulty in letting go. It is attached to always being right and trying to prove others wrong. It wants us to own possessions and people. Once we have something we want ego will then try to convince us that it's not enough and we need — must have — more, bigger, newer, faster, better.

Attachment — to people or things or ideas — is the antithesis of love. It demonstrates our belief in shortage. By being attached to someone we are stifling them, not allowing them the freedom they need in order to grow. And we are not allowing ourselves the space to grow either. We are trying to define the way they 'ought' to be. It is a form of dependency that is not healthy for either party.

### Example

Roy had very high expectations, both for other people and himself. He was always the first to complain when he did not receive the service he expected, if someone broke a promise, failed to return a phone call, or if his post went missing or was delivered late. He almost expected people to 'fail' him and would be on the phone or writing a letter as soon as something went 'wrong'. He was often scathing in his attacks, and although he often got what he called 'a result', it won him no friends. He wouldn't have been surprised if his complaints had resulted in at least one person getting the sack.

Once he took to the path of enlightenment, Roy realised that his reactions were unhelpful to say the least. He knew he was helping to create discord rather than harmony in the world. That his motives were more an ego-based need always to be right rather than being of service to others, which in his heart he knew to be his calling. He began to realise that by respecting the humanity of those involved he was able to accept that we all make mistakes; he certainly didn't need reminding of his own! As he became easier on himself he found he also became less critical of what he saw as the shortcomings of others. It didn't mean he stopped complaining when he felt it was justified, but he found he was more patient with other people, and when he did complain it was done politely and constructively in a way that enabled those concerned to retain their dignity and helped them improve the quality of their service to others.

### Exercise

Here is an exercise that will help you release some of your ego's negative programming. Each night just before you go to bed give a little thought to all the things you have achieved during the day. They need not be big things. They may be things you do every day and simply take for granted and have never acknowledged yourself for: phoning your mother, perhaps, or taking in a parcel for a neighbour.

Look at yourself in a mirror; look yourself right in the eyes. This can be scary for some people, looking yourself in the eyes; the eyes, as they say, are the gateway to the soul. Keep looking yourself in the eyes and then say, "[your name] I acknowledge you for..." and list all the things you've achieved during the day. Do this every evening for two months — and experience the change in the way you see yourself.

When you start to do this exercise, notice how you are feeling. How easy is it to look yourself in the eyes? How do you feel about acknowledging yourself? How easy was it to find things to acknowledge yourself for? You may wish to jot down in your notebook your feelings and perhaps discuss them with your special friend or buddy if you are working with someone else. After about a week, notice how you are feeling now and how this differs from a week earlier.

❖

# Life Purpose

As mentioned earlier, each of us is here on Earth at this time for a specific purpose. The apparently random events in our lives are actually part of a bigger plan. When we look back on our lives we can usually see patterns or distinct episodes. We can often see at the end of each episode of our lives how things have fitted together and how the events of that episode begin to make sense.

What goes on between each of our lives on Earth, when we are in the spirit realms, is probably not for us to know right now. However, one thing seems to be clear, that we make plans and arrangements for our next incarnation. This includes deciding what lessons we wish to learn and what experiences we wish to have, as well as agreeing with other souls who will support us in these activities. It also involves devising a 'life purpose' or Divine Plan for our life — what service we intend to be to humankind.

Our life purpose is one of those things we 'forget' when we incarnate on the Earth plane, or maybe in childhood. It is something most of have to work on in order to bring it back to our consciousness so we can be sure we are carrying it out to the best of our ability. That is not to say we are not fulfilling our purpose when we are not conscious of it, only that we are better able to accomplish our mission once we become consciously aware of what it is.

Knowing our Divine Plan does not necessarily mean we must give up the life we have now, fly off to some remote part of the planet and become missionaries, or retrain as counsellors, therapists, healers, teachers, trainers or life coaches, or give all our money to charity. Of course, for some people, it might mean just that. For others, it may mean continuing with their present occupations and spending some of their time helping out with a charity or community project, or tithing part of their income to a worthy cause. It may mean continuing one's present job and lifestyle with a different emphasis, perhaps focussing on ethical business, care and compassion for the consumer and the environment. But there again, we may have been living that kind of life all along and simply required confirmation.

Discovering what our life's purpose is can actually give purpose to our life. And, yes, if that sounds like a tautology, that's probably because it is! Perhaps more correctly, it puts purpose back into our life. So many of us find ourselves, professionally and personally, doing things to suit the whims of others — our parents, teachers, lovers, friends, boss, parish priest or society — that we lose touch with what we really want in life; with what really motivates us.

Now is the time to relearn what it is we are here to do. The chances are it is what we wanted to do from the beginning before we allowed others — our parents, teachers, friends — to steer us onto some other course. Something we were told was 'not suitable' for a young lady or young man, or would not earn us a living, was too dangerous, or whatever. Quite possibly it may involve us being more creative, less 'tied down' to a nine-to-five job, more involved with people. We will know when we rediscover it.

### Example

Cleo attended a workshop to help her rediscover her life's purpose. During a guided meditation in the workshop she visualised herself on a journey. She was guided through a luscious forest where she eventually met with an elderly, gnarled, hooded figure in a clearing. Cleo instinctively knew this was someone important to her even though she didn't see a face and didn't even know if they were male or female. As she approached this figure, the old person offered her a bag. Cleo took the bag and thanked the shrouded person, still unaware of whether they were male or female, or the identity of the figure. She opened the bag and saw inside an assortment of crystals. Cleo was surprised, not knowing anything about crystals other than that they were sometimes used for healing. Although she couldn't explain how or why, she realised this was a reminder that the purpose of her life was to heal her own past and help others to heal theirs.

After the meditation when the participants each shared their experiences in the meditation, Cleo expressed her surprise at what she learned, and said she was unsure of how she was supposed to react to this. The workshop leader pointed out that this did not necessarily mean Cleo was to give up her work with computers and become a healer, although she may wish to do that eventually. More likely it meant she was to work on healing herself, and possibly bring a healing aspect into her present work. Whatever it meant, the meaning would come clear to her if she continued to meditate and if she followed her intuition.

### Exercise

Find yourself somewhere quiet and peaceful where you wont be disturbed. Sit down and take a deep breath. Breathe is as far as you can, hold your breath for a few seconds and then breathe out slowly. Repeat this a few times and feel yourself relax deeper and deeper each time. Allow both your body and your mind relax.

Then in your notebook make a list of all the things you can do and all the things you enjoy doing; note that these may not necessarily be the same things. Include all the things you've been trained to do, both professionally and by attending personal training courses, your interests, hobbies, things you've taught yourself to do, serious and fun things. Don't leave anything out. Don't forget things that are not likely to earn you a living like eating, having sex, playing computer games. Also write down things you would like to do that you've never done before, and things you'd like to achieve. Give yourself between twenty and thirty minutes and keep writing whatever comes into your head. It is important to keep going and not allow your mind to get in the way and censor what you are writing.

When you have finished, review the list. Highlight those things you've not done for a while. Then write down on a separate page three or four of the items from those you've highlighted that you most want to do. Don't select them on the basis of which might be the easiest to do, but choose those you genuinely would most like to do. Now make plans to do those things. For each one write down things you need to do or things that need to be in place before you can achieve your goal. Next write a date beside each activity or each final result. Write the first date that comes to mind — do not try to censor your thoughts, just trust. Now you have a 'fun plan', something to start putting into action to enable you to regain more enjoyment and a better balance in your life.

Next, highlight in a different colour the things you really want to achieve in your life. Again, select three or four from those you've highlighted and go through the same process as above. Identify the three or four items you most wish to achieve and a series of actions and activities to help you achieve them, together with dates you will achieve them by. You now have a plan that, if not your complete life's purpose, at least has many elements of your life plan. Go out and do it!

You might wish to share anything you have learned with your special friend.

❖

# Peace

Peace — whether by this we mean world peace or an inner, personal, peace — begins with each one of us. When we feel calm and at ease with ourselves this inner peace is radiated out to all those around us.

Contentment, peace, inner calm, comes from accepting things just as they are without attempting to change them or even wishing to change them, without judging them as 'right' or 'wrong', or 'good' or 'bad'. With enlightenment comes acceptance of the perfection of each and every event and circumstance, even when the outcome is different from what we hoped for or expected, and even when we don't understand the reason or meaning of the event. A recognition that we cannot change the past, that the future will take care of itself and that all we have is *now*.

Peace is to do with so many things: an end to racial hatred, wife-bashing, child abuse, neighbour disputes, road rage, vandalism, homelessness, poverty, murders, theft, greed, desperation, an end to wars, an end to the nuclear arms race. More than this, it is about neighbours, strangers and nations getting on together and even helping each other, working for a common good rather than individual agendas.

We can only truly achieve a state of inner peace by uncovering, facing up to and finally resolving and healing our own buried fears, anxieties, frustrations, hurts and emotional scars. There is a distinct difference between what has been resolved and what we have simply buried. Something that has simply been buried will almost certainly resurface at some stage. Probably when we least expect it we will be faced with a 'trigger' that recalls that past hurt or fear and invites us to heal it. As always we have a choice. If we choose simply to bury it again, then it will surely resurface again and again until we eventually heal it.

When we begin to experience calm and peace within our lives we find we no longer care or worry about what other people may think about us, we don't need the approval of others, we stop looking behind us to see what others are doing. This is not to say that we do not care about other people; nor does it mean we conduct ourselves with impunity. Rather, we have greater compassion for others and we trust ourselves more, and we know instinctively that we are in the 'right' place at the 'right' time doing the 'right' thing. It frees us to enjoy our lives without constantly looking over our shoulders.

At the same time as we are working on our own inner peace, it is most important that we also work on issues such as world peace, an end to conflicts in strife-torn areas of the world, an end to poverty, starvation, homelessness, and a resolution to issues such as global warming. We may do so through prayer, meditation and visualisation. We should take care not to talk down such issues as being insoluble nor lose heart that our prayers are not being answered. Our prayers for such issues are important. However, rather than being answered immediately, the energy of our prayers, meditations and visualisations is combined with that of other lightworkers and others of goodwill until there is sufficient energy and will within the world to bring about the required change. Furthermore such changes are often made gradually in small steps.

### Example

Standing in a long, slow-moving queue at the Post Office one day, David noticed that several people ahead of him were beginning to get impatient. Some were sighing audibly or mumbling under their breath or groaning when someone at the counter took longer than they felt was warranted. The cashier, aware of the discontentment but knowing he was doing his best, felt unappreciated and was often short with the customers which only added to the malaise.

At first David was tempted to join in with the mumbling and grumbling. However, he caught himself in time, realising that his higher self was encouraging him to keep calm and keep his peace. He quietly centred himself, visualised a peaceful queue and asked for the assistance of his spirit guides. More than simply not adding to the frustrations of the queue, his positive attitude was contagious and seemed to raise the spirits of most of those around him. When he reached the counter David greeted the frazzled cashier with a smile, which was met at first with a look of surprise, almost of suspicion. But then his smile was returned and they exchanged a few pleasantries which went even further to lightening the atmosphere.

### Exercise

Most of us encounter frustrating events almost every day of our lives, perhaps with our partner or children, work colleagues, customers, suppliers, whilst driving on the roads, out shopping or just about anywhere. We might be tempted — and perhaps give in to the temptation — to shout, mutter under our breath, make a rude gesture or swear when we feel we have been provoked by the thoughtlessness or rudeness or arrogance of someone else.

Make a commitment to catch yourself at the point of temptation and not give in to the provocation. Instead of responding with an act or a word or a thought in kind, transmute the situation with an act or thought or word of love. Instead of responding from your lower ego, respond from your higher self. Maybe apologise, even though it was not your 'fault', or smile, or send a blessing or thoughts of love. Recognise that we are all spiritual beings at heart, perfect, whole and complete, that as humans we all make 'mistakes' and that it doesn't make us 'bad' people.

Having practised this for a week or two, share any insights you may have gained with your special friend if you wish.

# Intuition and Creativity

Once we are on the path of enlightenment we find we are more in touch with our intuition, that we start to allow ourselves more right brain activity. Our right brain is our intuitive and creative side, the part which urges us to act because something is intuitively right for us. On the other hand our left brain is our logical side, which encourages us to do nothing until we have all the facts and have thought about all the possibilities and permutations.

Most of us have learned to 'survive' in a competitive and what we perceive to be a dangerous world by repressing our right brain activity and using primarily our left brain. Many of us have lost our spontaneity, perhaps to the extent that we don't even believe we have it within us. Spirituality calls on us to reverse this process; to discard logic and calculated thought — or at least put it in its place — in favour of trusting our intuition, our spontaneity, our creativity.

How often have we felt an urge to do something, maybe take a different route home from work, buy that attractive dress, or whatever, only to have our left brain kick in and tell us not to be silly. 'You always go that way home; why go a different route?' 'Whatever do you want *another* new dress for?' Then a mile or so down the road we find ourselves in a massive traffic jam, and it's too late or too far to turn back. Or that very evening we receive a phone call from a friend inviting us to a party and *that* dress would have been just perfect for the occasion, and of course it's been sold when we go back the following day! That initial urge to do something different was our intuition speaking to us; it often speaks to us for a fraction of a second and if we're not careful our logical brain, our ego, gets in the way and thwarts our spontaneity and creativity.

There is intuition and creativity within all of us, not just a 'special' few; it is our birthright. Of course, we may not all wish to be an artist, a musician, writer, poet, potter, actor, healer, photographer, dancer or whatever by profession. However, many, perhaps most of us have an interest in one or more art forms from an amateur viewpoint.

The creative energy is all around us. It is simply a question of tuning into that energy, letting it flow through us and allowing it to work with us. We all have the ability to be creative in one way or another, whether this is in a professional way or simply for our own enjoyment, perhaps in gardening, cooking, home decoration or some other creative pastime.

Excessive tidiness can be a block to the creative energy, as can too much clutter, or too much thinking as these can block the flow of energy.

## Example

Jonathan was suffering with a problem — something he feels far too embarrassed about to have explained here. He was thinking about going to his doctor but wasn't keen on taking drugs at the best of times, and he felt that a more natural remedy would be available if only he knew where to turn for help. He didn't relish telling even his friends about his discomfort and didn't know where to turn for help. Then one Sunday while he was out walking he felt the urge to buy a Sunday newspaper — something he did only on rare occasions. He had been working hard all week as well as part of the weekend, so a relaxing afternoon just reading the paper would be very welcome, he figured. He was reading the 'problem page' and wondering at the predicament some people got themselves into when he noticed a letter from someone with a problem similar to his own. The counsellor recommended a book of herbal and natural remedies that seemed likely to cover his condition. Thanking the universe for its support, he promptly made a note of the title and ordered a copy the following day.

### Exercise

This is not the time to sit quietly in contemplation! Now would be a good time to get up and get out! Go for a walk. Yes, that's right — it's time for a walk! It's entirely up to you where you choose to go: perhaps to a local park or wood, beside the river, to the seaside, to a museum or art gallery, or even some busy market; somewhere familiar or somewhere new. Take with you your notebook and a pen, but go alone. You may wish to take a little money with you and if you're going to, or by a market, get yourself some small token. Or you may like to take your camera and shoot some photos, or take a sketchpad. But take no one else with you — human or animal — and do not speak to anyone, unless it is unavoidable. This is a time for you *with* you.

As you walk, notice the detail in everything around you, those details you might normally miss or take for granted: the shapes of the leaves, the trees, litter, buildings, stones, clouds, objects whether man-made or natural; notice the different colours and different shades of colour; sounds; the movement of objects; their texture and markings; smells and any feelings you may get.

Walk for about twenty to thirty minutes and then find somewhere to sit down and write. Write about whatever you noticed on your walk; describe the shapes, the colours, the sounds, the textures, etc. Consider how much of this you might have missed had you not been *actively* watching, looking, listening. Write about anything you have learned in the process.

You might wish to share what you have learned about yourself or about life with your partner or buddy or special friend.

❖

# Angels

Perhaps once we accept the idea that we are ourselves spiritual beings, it can be easier to believe that other unseen spiritual beings exist and to accept that they are able to communicate with us and we with them.

There are many 'orders' of beings of light and love, which include the ascended masters, angels and archangels, and spirits, and it is not within this book to write about them all or about any in great detail. However, we should all be aware that each of us has a companion angel — some people call them a guardian angel, but this suggests there is something we need to be guarded against, which is not the case — and a spirit guide, both of whom are there — or rather here — to help us if we call upon their assistance. It is important to know that they will only help us if we ask them. For them to do otherwise would be to interfere with our free will, and they will never do that.

These beings of love and light wish only to assist us in our journey of enlightenment. Once we connect with our companion angel and our spirit guides and invite them to help us, we will experience unexplained 'coincidences', things and people turning up in your life at just the right moment, we will find that so many things in life run just that much more smoothly, and we will feel more secure in the knowledge that we are in the right place at the right time doing the right thing.

Angels have a great sense of humour and appreciate being talked to and included in every part of our lives. We can tell them our hopes and wishes and our troubles without fear of judgement, and sometimes just talking to our friends can help us find a solution to a situation in which we are stuck.

Although they have been helping humankind throughout our evolution, angels are more active in our lives than at any other time in our history. There are many open human beings who consciously 'channel' messages from the angelic realms for the higher good of themselves and others. They may receive information in a number of different ways; perhaps through what is called 'automatic writing', through images — clairvoyance — or voices — clairaudience. Others — most of us — receive guidance and help in more subtle ways; through the words of a song or book or on the radio, or through some other apparently everyday activity.

## Example

This book would not have happened without the loving help of my friends 'upstairs', and they have my grateful thanks for all their assistance. I feel somewhat uneasy about calling the book my work given the amount of assistance they have given me. Some parts came directly during meditations; other parts — the majority — came by maintaining an open attitude, writing only when I felt like it, not trying to force the pace, and trusting my own intuition. At one point over a very short space of time I was given so many books to read, from a variety of sources, each of which contained one further piece of the 'puzzle' that was to be this book.

My own introduction to angels was through a channeller, Debra, who was later to become a good friend. At first I was puzzled and a little sceptical about the messages and the whole idea. However, I went along with most of the advice I was given, although my interpretation was sometime a little awry! A couple of years later I met a clairvoyant who was guided by angels in all departments of her life. She introduced me to some of the many ways in which angels work with humans to help us in our lives. At present, whilst I am aware of the important part 'them upstairs' (the affectionate, joking way I talk about my angel and spirit friends) play in my life and often sense a presence, I am not in any accepted way, nor do I consider myself to be, a channeller or medium.

### Exercise

It is very helpful before first making contact with our angel and spirit guides, and indeed at other times when we wish to attain states of higher consciousness to open our body's energy centres — or chakras. To do this find yourself a quiet space; play some soft music and light some candles and some incense. Make yourself comfortable in whatever position you find most suitable with your spine straight. Close your eyes. Breathe in as far as you can — and a little bit more. Hold your breath for several seconds and then breathe out slowly, allowing your body to relax as you do so. Repeat this a further three or four times, each time becoming more and more relaxed. Allow your mind to relax and clear of all thoughts.

Now, start to draw in energy from the base of your spine. One by one, allow the energy to move up your spine to each of your chakras in turn, opening them as it goes. Visualise the energy as a warm, bright, pulsating light. First, visualise your base chakra, a spot at the base of your spine, glowing with a deep red energy. Hold that energy for a while and allow your chakra open.

Still drawing in the energy from the base of your spine, let the energy move up to your sacral chakra, a couple of inches below your navel. See your sacral chakra glow with a warm orange energy. Again, hold the energy and let it open your chakra. When you are ready, feel the energy move on up to your solar plexus chakra and see it glow with a yellow energy. Allow the energy to open your chakra.

Remember to keep drawing in energy from your root chakra. Let it move up to your heart chakra, at the centre of your breastbone. See this glow with a green energy and feel your heart chakra open. Take your time. Next allow the energy to flow up to your thymus chakra, about halfway between your breastbone and your throat. See this glow with an aquamarine (turquoise) energy and let your chakra open. Then feel the energy move up to your throat chakra where it glows with a blue energy. Again, hold the energy for a moment and feel your chakra open. Draw the energy up to your third eye chakra, the centre of your forehead. Feel it glow with a dark blue (indigo) energy and feel your third eye chakra open. Finally, allow the energy to move up to your crown chakra. Feel it flow all the way up your spine. Feel your chakra open as it glows with a beautiful violet energy.

Allow the energy to flow out of the top of your head and cascade down your outer body cleansing as it goes.

Now using whatever words seem most fitting invite your companion angel into your heart to help you in your life; an example is given in the section entitled 'Prayer and Meditation – meet your angel', which you may use if you wish. If you want to you may specify where you most feel in need of assistance, but it may be best not to limit your friend. Don't talk too much. Your friend loves you talking to them, but this is not the time to say too much as you want to give yourself the opportunity to hear what they have to say to you. In the silence of your meditative state allow your angel to talk to you. Ask them what it is that you most need to know at this time. You may not hear any words; you may feel a warmth, or a feeling of peace come over you; you may hear or see or sense a name; or you may not sense much at all. Whatever you do feel is fine. Don't be hard on yourself or your angel if you did not experience much. Spend as long as you want in this state. When you are ready, thank your angel. You don't need to say 'goodbye' as they are with you all the time, whether you are conscious of the fact or not.

Having opened your chakras at the beginning of the process, you will now need to close them — all except your base chakra and your crown chakra. This can be a very quick exercise. To do this, first visualise your chakras as a rainbow of light all down your spine from violet at your crown, through indigo, blue, aquamarine, green, yellow and orange to red and your base chakra. Now visualise a white light coming from your crown chakra and running down the outside of your body. As it flows past each chakra allow it to close that chakra. Remember not to close your crown chakra or your base chakra.

# Prayer and Meditation

It is a thin line that distinguishes prayer from meditation. Both are concerned with contacting God, the universe, our higher selves and/or other divine beings. As a very general over-simplification prayer is often to do with *talking* whilst meditation is more about *listening*.

Prayer usually takes the form of annunciating our desires to the universe, or God, or whoever may be listening. These may be requests for personal favours, or more altruistic requests such as for healing or relief for individuals or communities, or for peace in troubled areas of the globe. Alternatively, we may meditate on or visualise an improvement in the situation we are seeking to influence. In these circumstances very often the effect is not immediate but is stored together with the prayers of many others in some form of collective prayer energy for future use. It is important that our prayers and meditations are directed for 'the highest good of all', which means we must not seek to interfere with someone else's free will, and that it must be for positive ends.

One of the main reasons for meditating is to quieten our ego-based thoughts and enable us to get in touch with our higher consciousness, our divine self. Our thoughts, our worries and our constant inner dialogue are some of the ways in which our ego tries to keep us from knowing our inner selves. Once we are able to quieten our thoughts and inner dialogue, we make it possible for our 'higher self' to make itself known. When meditating we may also make contact with our friends and loved ones who are in spirit, with our guides, or with the 'higher selves' of loved ones still on the Earth plane. Whatever 'comes through' is what we need to know at that time and it is important not to try and force this process — forcing it is our ego trying to impress its will on us.

Don't worry if nothing happens. The process of quietening the mind and inner dialogue can be a tough one and it takes practice. Don't give up; it is better to practise for just five minutes a day than to give up. Better still to practise for ten or twenty minutes! However, it would be better for the beginner to build up to it gradually rather than try and then give up. Meditation is not the only way in which to contact our 'higher selves'. It is a good place to start, although we should always be open to our intuition and spiritual guidance throughout the waking day as well as in our sleep. If you've ever had a flash of inspiration or a sudden impulse to phone someone then that has probably come from your 'higher self' or your guides.

### How to Meditate

There are almost as many ways in which to meditate as there are people who meditate! And there are many books teaching how to, or how not to meditate. They're all right — and they're all wrong! What is important is to find a way that works for you. No one finds meditating easy; it is reported that even the Dalai Lama has said he finds meditating difficult! So keep at it.

You may find it helpful to light some candles and an incense stick. Candles bring light into your space, whilst incense has a purifying effect. Both help to create a more peaceful and spiritual atmosphere for meditating. You may or may not wish to play some quiet music. Some people find guided, taped meditations to be helpful. Then again, you may feel like using different methods on different occasions; there may be times when you want background music, at other times just quiet; occasions when you want a guided meditation, other times not. Whatever suits you at the time.

Find a spot where you can get comfortable, whether sitting, kneeling, squatting or lying. Some books advise not to lie down to meditate partly because there is a danger of falling asleep. Others believe it is important for your feet to be in contact with the floor to give you 'grounding', and yet others advise sitting in a hard-back chair or keeping your spine straight. However, some people find meditating in bed, or even in the bath, to be most beneficial. Whilst it is important not to be so relaxed that you fall asleep, there really are no rights and wrongs, just whatever suits you best.

The following is offered as a suggestion to get you started. If it works for you then feel free to use it; if not, feel free to experiment until you find something that does help.

When you are ready and in a comfortable position, breathe deeply several times. Breathe in as deeply as you can; hold your breath for several seconds before breathing out again, slowly. Relax your mind; let go of any thoughts that are there. Then start to relax your body, starting from your head and working down to your toes, or starting at your feet and working upwards. As you breathe out, feel the tension flow out of your body through the soles of your feet. Visualise roots growing out from the soles of your feet and from the base of your spine (your root chakra); see them growing deep within the earth. When they are as deep as they will go, start to draw in energy from the earth through your roots; loving, powerful, grounding energy. Feel it fill your entire body. Be aware of your breathing and take even breaths in and out, in and out.

Where you go from here is entirely up to you. It is important to focus your mind on something in order to keep it from wandering and imposing its ideas on your meditation. One of the most common ways to do this is to count your breaths; another is with a visualisation, or to keep repeating a mantra. You may wish to go on a journey through woods and forests, by a stream, or by the seaside, perhaps meeting with people who may have a message or a gift for you; you may wish to bring healing to friends and to the peoples and places of the world that are in turmoil and in need of healing; or you may just wish to be still and just focus on your breath or the flame of a candle.

You may find — in fact you almost certainly will find —

that your mind will start to wander from time to time. Don't castigate yourself, this is a perfectly human occurrence. You're not 'bad', or 'wrong', or a 'failure'! Just be aware of the thought and let it go, thanking it and telling it lovingly it's not wanted right now. With practice you will often be able to stop your thoughts before they emerge, which will lead to a greater depth of meditating.

Another form of meditation is to spend between twenty and thirty minutes each day — preferably at the very beginning of the day — writing. Writing whatever comes into your mind. It might be gripes and moans, hopes and desires, complete drivel. If you can think of nothing to write, then simply write, 'I don't know what to write today' and keep writing it until something flows. Whatever it is, write it down. Keep going. Write without thinking and without stopping.

This may not seem much like meditating; it may even seem like a complete waste of time. Certainly for the first few mornings of writing nothing much is likely to happen. However, after several days, or maybe weeks, you may begin to find something starting to appear. Words, phrases, perhaps even several sentences may begin to appear on the page that came quite unexpectedly. It could be a feeling you've kept hidden, a thought of an old friend who you decide to contact, an idea that leads to a new job, the beginning of a poem or short story. You may find yourself thinking, 'Where did that come from?' The answer is, it came from your subconscious. It is real, something to take seriously and something to be thankful for.

This kind of writing helps you get behind the illusions you create for yourself, and get in touch with your subconscious, which is what meditating is about.

### A Group Meditation

The following meditation may be useful as it stands for a group situation, or with some modification when alone.

Sit still. Put your hands on your knees. Relax your body, starting with your feet and moving slowly up to your legs, your thighs, your torso, your arms, neck, and your head. Now start to relax your mind. Forget all that has been going on for you before this moment, your journey here, meeting with old friends, meeting new people. Whatever is in your mind, just let it go.

If any thoughts come into your mind, thank them and tell them with love they're not wanted right now. Become aware of the presence of God, and of your companion angel, who is with you at all times. Acknowledge your angel. Be aware of your connectedness with everyone in the room, and with all of humanity, and with the entire universe.

Recognise that your purpose for being on Earth at this time is to experience and to help others experience their connectedness.

Visualise your heart as a beautiful pale pink energy, the pink of unconditional love. See it getting bigger and bigger, encompassing everyone in the room, filling them with your love. See it encompassing all the towns and countryside around until it fills the whole country. And it still keeps on growing till it fills the Earth, sharing your love with everyone and everything, especially those you most resist — maybe the homeless, politicians, landowners, the rich, the poor, liars and cheats, terrorists, people in war-torn parts of the world, those suffering from natural disasters, rapists, your friends, your families, spiders, snakes, dog mess on the pavement... — fill in your own pet loves and hates, remembering they are all part of God's wonderful creation. Just visualise this beautiful pale pink energy of your love bringing a sense of connectedness to the whole planet, and focus your thoughts on harmony reigning throughout the world.

When you are ready, bring yourself back to the room and open your eyes.

### A Healing Meditation

The following meditation is offered to bring healing to individuals or troubled areas of the world.

Begin by relaxing and grounding yourself, using whatever technique works best for you.

Then visualise your heart as a beautiful pink energy within you, the colour that represents unconditional love. See the energy start to expand, and as it grows visualise it move outside your body. See it move away from you in front of you where you can see it clearly as it continues to grow.

Just look at it, knowing it is your heart full of the Divine love you have to share. Now, one by one, take those people you care about who are in need of healing and place them into your heart. As you watch, see the difference your love is making to them. See them healing in front of your eyes.

Take your time. Take each person you know who needs healing into your heart and watch them heal. Once you have taken all those you know into your heart, start to take those you know of only through the newspapers or media who need healing, the starving nations of the world, those caught up in conflicts. Remember, your heart is big enough for them all.

Visualise world starvation and conflicts begin to dissolve before your very eyes as they are surrounded and fed by your love. Hold that picture knowing with gratitude that you have brought peace and healing to millions of people throughout the world.

When you are ready, bring yourself back to the room and open your eyes.

### Meet Your Angel

If we wish to connect with our guides we have only to ask. A simple invocation inviting them into our life is all that is required, as well as being in a receptive state of mind. We may invite them directly, or we may ask for the assistance of a connecting angel. The following prayer may be useful, or we may use whatever words seem most appropriate to us at the time:

> *Blessed friends of love and light, I ask you to support me on my spiritual journey. Help me to be open to, and hear and*

understand your guidance throughout my life, and I ask for your patience when I seem to miss the message. I value your love and friendship, and ask only that I may be of service to humankind.

### Protection

As you begin to open yourself to the infinite wisdom of the universe, as the light within you starts to grow, you will find you become more sensitive to the energies all around you. As a result you will probably need to protect yourself from negative energies both from people around you as well as from those in spirit that are confused and will seek out any source of light, like moths, or that are out to cause mischief or create confusion.

There are many ways in which to protect yourself from such energies, including visualisations and meditations, or calling upon the assistance of spiritual beings on other planes. It is arguably better to use both a meditation or visualisation as well as an invocation, since the former is helping to develop your own powers; however, in an emergency where time is critical, a simple invocation will suffice.

A simple visualisation to protect yourself is to picture yourself surrounded by a cloud of golden light. See yourself within the protective haze of energy and hold the image for a few seconds.

The following is a simple invocation for the assistance of archangel Michael for the purpose of protection:

*Lord Michael before me*
*Lord Michael behind me*
*Lord Michael to the left of me*
*Lord Michael to the right of me*
*Lord Michael above me*
*Lord Michael below me*
*Lord Michael protect me. Lord Michael protect me. Lord Michael protect me.*
*Thank you. Thank you. Thank you.*

An alternative invocation is to repeat three times:

*Under Universal Law, I call upon the Gold Ray of Christ for my total protection.*

followed by

*It is done; it is done; it is done.*

❖

# Inspirational Quotes

May the following quotes speak to your heart in whatever way you choose to interpret them.

*Great men are they who see that spiritual is stronger than any material force, that thoughts rule the world.*
Ralph Waldo Emerson

*Enlightenment demands that you take responsibility for your way of life.*
Wayne Dyer

*Whether you believe you can do a thing or you believe you can't, you're right.*
Henry Ford

*Instructions for life:*
*1. Take into account that great love and great achievements involve great risk.*
*2. When you lose, don't lose the lesson.*
*3. Follow the three Rs: Respect for self; Respect for others, and Responsibility for all your actions.*
*4. Remember that not getting what you want is sometimes a wonderful stroke of luck.*
*5. Learn the rules so you know how to break them properly.*
*6. Don't let a little dispute injure a great friendship.*
*7. When you realize you've made a mistake, take immediate steps to correct it.*
*8. Spend some time alone every day.*

*9. Open your arms to change, but don't let go of your values.*
*10. Remember that silence is sometimes the best answer.*
*11. Live a good, honourable life. Then when you get older and think back, you'll be able to enjoy it a second time.*
*12. A loving atmosphere in your home is the foundation for your life.*
*13. In disagreements with loved ones, deal only with the current situation. Don't bring up the past.*
*14. Share your knowledge. It's a way to achieve immortality.*
*15. Be gentle with the earth.*
*16. Once a year, go someplace you've never been before.*
*17. Remember that the best relationship is one in which your love for each other exceeds your need for each other.*
*18. Judge your success by what you had to give up in order to get it.*
*19. Approach love and cooking with reckless abandon.*

Attributed to the Dalai Lama

*Until one is committed, there is the chance to draw back; always ineffectiveness. Concerning all acts of initiative (and creation) there is one elementary truth, the ignorance of which kills countless ideas and splendid plans; that the moment one definitely commits oneself, then Providence moves too. All sorts of things occur to help one that would never otherwise have occurred. A whole stream of events issues from the decision, raising in one's favour all manner of unforeseen incidents and meetings and material assistance which no man could have dreamed would come his way. I have learned a deep respect for one of Goethe's couplets: "Whatever you can do, or dream you can, begin it. Boldness has genius, power and magic in it."*

W H Murray, Scottish Himalayan Expedition

*People intuitively understand that a good business enhances the lives of all who work within it, and enriches the lives of all those who are touched by it. Likewise, the business you can succeed with is distinctly and utterly you and yours. It is unlike any other business in the world. Being in business is not about making money. It is a way to become who you are.*

Paul Hawkins

*I sit on a man's back, choking him and making him carry me, and yet assure myself and others that I am very sorry for him and wish to ease his lot by all possible means - except by getting off his back.*

Leo Tolstoy

*Our deepest fear is not that we are inadequate. Our deepest fear is that we are powerful beyond measure. It is our light, not our darkness, that most frightens us. We ask ourselves, who am I to be brilliant, gorgeous, talented, fabulous? Actually, who are you NOT to be? You are a child of God. Your playing small does not serve the world. There is nothing enlightening about shrinking so that other people won't feel unsure around you. We were born to make manifest the glory of God that is within us. It is not just in some of us; it is in everyone. As we let our own light shine, we unconsciously give other people permission to do the same. As we are liberated from our own fear, our presence automatically liberates others.*

Nelson Mandela

*Lord, make me an instrument of your peace. Where there is hatred let me bring love. Where there is injury, pardon. Where there is doubt, faith. Where there is despair, hope. Where there is darkness, light. And where there is sadness let me bring joy.*

Saint Francis of Assisi

*In my world nothing ever goes wrong.*

Anon

*Go — not knowing where. Bring — not knowing what. The path is long, the way unknown.*

Russian Fairy Tale

*Abnormal people are the only people who have ever changed the world… Because normal people stay normal.*

David M. Hasz

*The position of the artist is humble. He is essentially a channel.*

Piet Mondrian